GW01100178

Setting Up In Spain

Setting Up In Spain

David Hewson

MEREHURST
—LONDON—

Published 1990 by Merehurst Limited
Ferry House, 51-57 Lacy Road
Putney, London SW15 1PR

Copyright © David Hewson 1990

ISBN 1 85391 083 X

Designed and produced by Snap! Books
Typeset by David Hewson and TRS Graphics
Maps by Lovell Johns, Long Hanborough, Oxfordshire
Printed in Great Britain by Mackays of Chatham plc, Chatham, Kent

All rights reserved. No part of this publication may
be reproduced, stored in a retrieval system, or
transmitted by any form or by any means,
electronic, mechanical, photocopying, recording or
otherwise, without written permission of
Merehurst Limited and the copyright holder.

Contents

Introduction

1 Setting the Scene	5
Map of Spain	20
2 The Regions of Spain	21
Map of Costa del Sol	22
3 Finding a Home	48
4 Buying Spanish Property	52
5 Renting Property	70
6 Timeshare Properties	73
7 Residency and Working	91
8 Arranging your Finances	112
9 Everyday Life	120
Bibliography	133
Sources of Information	135
Glossary of Useful Terms	155
Index	157

Introduction

'Round and round the spicy downs the yellow
Lotos-dust is blown.'
                    The Lotos-Eaters, Alfred Lord Tennyson

There is a touch of the lotus-eater in every one of us, and nowhere does the 'Lotos-dust' blow more fragrantly than along the coastline of Spain. Holidays beguile with tantalising dreams which dawn faintly and grow ever more real as the dread day of return looms. Why leave this heavenly climate for the damp and cold of home? Why desert the sea and sand, the food and wine, the Mediterranean way of life for the drab existence of northern Europe? And, from these hazy beginnings, the plans for timeshare, a second property, and perhaps a permanent move to live and work begin to grow.

During the next decade, as national frontiers fade, the continued development of Spain's more popular regions into bustling international communities seems beyond question. The climate is admirable, the people friendly, particularly towards those who learn a little of their language, and the culture vivid yet familiar.

Around 200,000 Britons now have a home in Spain, most of them in Andalucia, the Canary Islands, or in the Balearics, and they are joined by many thousands more people from northern Europe each year. In some ways, the familiar strip of Costa del Sol coastline running from Málaga to Gibraltar has ceased to be part of Spain, and become, instead, a cosmopolitan community in which English pubs live cheek by jowl with traditional *bodegas*, and the odd mosque for rich Arab visitors brushes against a Church of England meeting hall.

Yet this boom has not been without its victims. An English member of the European Parliament, Edward McMillan-Scott, who has taken a particular interest in Spanish property matters, reported to the Parliament in January 1989:

> 'For the great majority of foreign property buyers, while the procedures may seem strange and slow, no significant problems arise. But for a substantial minority, their dream of a home in the sun becomes a nightmare from which they are unable to escape. At worst they lose their villa or flat and their entire life savings through fraud and inefficiency or almost always because of their failure to take legal advice. At best they find themselves involved in unending bureaucratic entanglements.'

The difficulties facing anyone moving to Spain are real. But they should not be exaggerated, nor should it be forgotten that many stem from the folly of the intending purchaser. Most foreigners who have bought property have never looked back. A number have experienced small problems; a minority have regretted that they ever considered the idea. With common sense and good professional advice, it is possible to buy property in Spain without risk. Purchases made on impulse, or ones in which short cuts have been taken in order to save a few pounds, are, on the other hand, very dangerous indeed.

The Spanish property market, like many others, is no stranger to high pressure selling, dubious contracts, and hidden charges or debts. While most of those practising such tricks are not Spanish themselves, the nation's legal framework is ill equipped to deal with the special problems posed by foreign property transactions. The problem was summed up by the Spanish consumer organisation, the Defensor del Pueblo, in a report to the Spanish Prime Minister in 1987:

> 'It has been said that the foreign victims of property frauds share part of the blame for not taking advice prior to embarking on the purchase of property, from either the relevant public authorities or appropriate professional advisers; it has also been said that the developers, or those responsible for such painful situations, are themselves

often foreigners. All of this is true, but in many cases the losses incurred have to be laid at the door of deficiencies in the legal provisions governing the property market and the inadequacy of the administrative structure responsible for monitoring them, especially in the case of the smaller local authorities. For this reason, as well as legal measures to control the property market in Spain, there is a need for special additional measures specifically geared to foreign buyers or owners.'

Nor, all too often, do those planning to live permanently in Spain look much beyond the beauty of a summer's day when thinking of what life in another country really means. What happens if you fall ill? How will you make new friends? Are you in debt to the English or the Spanish taxman, or both? How will you cope with the death of a partner? And will the daily round of sun, sand and siesta begin to pall after a few months?

A home in the sun can be a life-enhancing experience for an active retired couple. It can also mean loneliness and bitter regrets at what has been left behind for those who never took the time to consider the realities of life abroad.

This book is not designed to replace the services of a trained professional. A reliable lawyer is essential for anyone contemplating a property purchase in Spain, or any other country for that matter. This is a message which many prospective purchasers ignore, to their peril. I have tried to set out here guidelines which should enable you to find good advice, and to monitor whether your professional representatives are performing the tasks you require of them. Just as important, I have tried to pose some of the questions which should be asked by anyone who is seriously thinking of living in Spain – many of which are questions which should be asked of oneself.

Lest the warnings here tend to overshadow the subject, let me stress at the beginning: the benefits, for those who are conscientious, more than outweigh the chore of precautions. Spain is a marvellous and rewarding place for a first or second home, provided you know what you are doing, and what to expect when your sale is finalised and the keys to your new villa or apartment are handed over.

Some of the topics covered by this book will be changed by the harmonisation of inter-government rules of EEC member states in 1992. This much-vaunted date is meant to introduce the free movement of capital and labour throughout Europe. If this occurs to plan, then the present restrictions on work permits and currency exchange will disappear. The detail of precisely what will happen between member states in 1992 is unlikely to be made clear until very close to the date itself, however, and there are many, including the author, who feel that the reality will, at least for a few years, be somewhat less sweeping than the intention. Two things can be said about 1992 with some certainty: the event *will* make it easier for EEC nationals to buy property and live in Spain. And whatever concessions are introduced, they are unlikely to be retrospective. It would be foolish to break the law of today in the expectation that the regulations of tomorrow will legalise your actions. In practice, this *may* be the case, but you will be taking a risk.

Researching a book of this nature requires the patient help of many people. I would particularly like to thank the following for their assistance: Geoff Brown of the National Westminster Bank European Business section; Charlotte Fenn, Spanish National Tourist Office; Edward McMillan-Scott, Member of the European Parliament; the Consumers' Association; the Timeshare Developers Association; Anna Skidmore, Mallorca; and the indefatigable staff of the Tropicana Hotel, Torremolinos, who, as always, were a perpetual source of support and advice while I was researching the book.

I am also indebted to the many foreign residents of La Carihuela, Torremolinos, who were more than happy to retell their experiences of living in Spain, good and bad, to a complete stranger full of largely impertinent questions.

They taught me that some of the wisest words on buying property in Spain can be found in whatever watering holes the local expatriates use in the locality, a lesson the prospective purchaser would do well to take to heart.

1 Setting the Scene

These are changing times for anyone who has ever cast an envious eye on a castle, a villa, or even a small apartment in Spain. Subtle shifts in work and leisure patterns in Europe no longer confine the right to live abroad to a very wealthy few. A combination of factors, technological, social and economic, have opened up the Mediterranean coastline to a new generation of residents seeking a relaxed carefree life in the sun, if only for a few months of the year.

Fax machines and computers have created innovative ways of earning a living without being tied to the office or factory. In Spain today, north European businessmen run businesses in their home countries through the simple modern expedients of the fax machine and the personal computer installed in a room of their Mediterranean villa.

The technology involved is relatively inexpensive yet brings to the expatriate businessman powers which, five years ago, were not available in the most advanced conventional office, such as the ability to switch currency into different accounts, to check precisely on bank balances, and pay wages, seven days a week, 24 hours a day.

Spain's *Lookout* magazine, the most influential English language publication in the country, documented, in February 1989, the lifestyles of several of this new generation of international workers. One was a taxi driver who spent half his time by the Mediterranean and the rest driving a London cab. Another was an oil platform worker who commuted monthly from Málaga to Aberdeen. A third ran a catering business in southern England

and a property company in Spain from his permanent home on the Costa del Sol.

At the same time, patterns of traditional work are changing. Staff employees receive longer and more flexible holidays which give them the time to enjoy a foreign property. In many sectors, there is a shift towards self employment and small business creation which further releases those involved from the conventional pressures of a 9 to 5, Monday to Friday week. Rising property prices in the United Kingdom have given many homeowners a residual property value which goes far beyond any sum which they might have saved in a bank deposit scheme through normal means; more and more are realising that value and using the balance to buy a home in the sun and sufficient investment income to pay for their day-to-day needs.

For those who cannot afford outright purchase, timeshare, though controversial and not without drawbacks, and inexpensive long term rentals have provided ways of finding temporary homes which are a feasible alternative to package holiday hotels.

This trend can only continue in the years to come. Air fares throughout Europe are, in real terms, lower than they were a decade ago, and likely to fall still further as airline deregulation and the Channel Tunnel bring yet more competition. The package holiday boom of the 1960s and 1970s created an appetite for the Mediterranean and Spain in particular among north Europeans. It is plain that the satisfied package holidaymakers of last year are the villa, apartment and timeshare purchasers of this – a trend which is already beginning to worry Spanish hotel companies who have complained to their Government that timeshare in particular is in direct and unfair competition to their traditional trade.

There are many different kinds of homes in Spain – from the £5,000 timeshare unit to the £15,000 resort studio, from the inexpensive converted farmhouse in a rural area away from the coast to the luxury villa by a fashionable resort which may cost £250,000. Yet in some ways the *kind* of home you seek is less important than the reasons why you are seeking it. If the notion of a home in Spain is beginning to grip you, ask yourself: why? The real answer is rarely as simple as it might seem – the climate, the food, the sea. Or at least it *shouldn't* be.

The most unfortunate people of all are those who fall in love with a view, a village or a simplistic picture of life beside the Mediterranean and then take the plunge without much more than a moment's thought. For them, Spain is simply a picture postcard come true in which the sun always shines, the locals are always friendly, and the cares of life which seem so apparent at home vanish the moment one arrives. It is an utterly false picture, of course, as they soon discover that a holiday which is permanent is no longer a holiday.

Buying a home abroad for the first time – whether it is a time-share apartment or a luxury villa – should be enjoyable, exhausting *and* instructive, a voyage of discovery in which the unexplored land is yourself just as much as your chosen country. Only an estate agent can listen to your requirements for 30 seconds and then declare, 'I have just the *perfect* place for you'. Mere mortals can offer no such advice. *You* know whether a home is really perfect for you, though you may not wish to admit it. Home-hunting of any kind is a heart-stopping mixture of self-deception and basic truths.

The properties which seem ideal are, invariably, the ones which are just out of your reach. And can you really turn a blind eye to that development being started around the corner just because the villa you've found looks so delightful in itself? You may tell yourself that what you really want is a home in 'real' Spain, in an out-of-the-way village where not a word of English is heard. But do you really want to pass up the superb facilities which can be found in most modern resorts, good shops and supermarkets which surpass many in France for their range of fine foods? And will you honestly learn sufficient Spanish to keep up with the machine-gun chatter of your new neighbours?

If you are serious about spending a substantial amount of time in Spain, you need to examine your real motives very closely. It is all very well to feel that you want to be near the heart of Spanish culture, but if the truth is that you'd like a relaxing home near the beach where you can pick up English newspapers easily and dine out in a different cuisine nightly, the joys of your mountain mansion may soon start to wear thin. On the other hand, if your main aim in retirement is to sit down and write a best-seller in utter peace and quiet, a frontline apartment in Marbella, with all its attendant distractions, will guarantee a severe case of writer's block as surely as anything.

Spain can also be mightily deceptive about the true nature of its very varied communities. That little bungalow in a mountain village might look idyllic. But if it is next to the local bar you will often be listening to the raucous chatter of the neighbourhood well into the early hours. There is no concept of noise as pollution in Spain, as anyone who lives next to a garrulous Spanish family will discover. During the many fiestas, hardly a soul sleeps, which is all very well for one night but a little wearing when the festivities go on for a week. Everyone has heard of Holy Week celebrations in Spain; it is worth remembering that Spanish travel agents also organise Holy Week 'escape breaks' for people who want to close their eyes and sleep for a few hours over Easter.

Equally, some of the busy resort areas have their surprises, small residential areas which are quiet, yet have gregarious communities with shops and restaurants open all year. La Carihuela, the old fishing village which was once the main street of Torremolinos, is just such an area, almost indistinguishable to the casual visitor, surrounded as it is by the bustling, modern high rise resorts of Benalmadena and new Torremolinos. La Carihuela is an indication of another novel aspect of contemporary Spain: the very localised effect of tourist development. However large the resort, however much it seems overwhelmed by English, German or Scandinavian influences, you can guarantee that a village only a few miles distant will be leading life much as it always did. Spain is never far distant, even in the most cosmopolitan of beach towns.

The first-time buyer who is looking to spend many years in Spain, even if it is only for a few weeks at a time, should feel in no hurry to find the perfect 'place in the hills'. Personally, I would recommend a home in or close to an established international community as a first stepping stone into Spain. It is easier to begin at the centre and work out than to start, from scratch, in a remote location. It is simpler to graduate from an established location, learning the language, getting to know more about Spain and your locality, and making new friends, and then moving to a house in the country, than to begin in rural isolation, however splendid it may be, from day one.

But there can be no rules for this sort of thing. Many people have bought broken down, deserted farmhouses in the wilds behind the Costa del Sol and turned them into luxury homes. Given the increasing popularity of rural villas, they probably stand to make a genuine and substantial profit out of their transaction when they come to sell – something that cannot be said of too many properties in established locations.

It is a question of choice and personality. In other words...

WHAT SORT OF BUYER ARE YOU?

Your choice of home will be determined by two factors. The first is financial – how much do you want to spend, and how willing are you to borrow the money if necessary? The second is personal – why, precisely, do you want a home in Spain, and what do you expect it to give you. Essentially, there are three kinds of buyers involved in the Spanish market.

Someone who wants a holiday home

The traditional foreign buyer in Spain fits into this category. Most will be looking for properties in coastal tourist areas well served by English-speaking estate agencies.

Someone who wants to retire

Increasingly, couples are using the value of large homes in Britain to pay for retirement homes in Spain, some as primary residences, others to be used as second homes rotated with a smaller property in the home country.

Someone who wants to work

Whether you want to run a bar in Tenerife or an investment company in Marbella, your choice of home as a worker in Spain becomes more complex than either of the other two categories. Investment value, schooling, and the local economy are among the factors which need careful consideration... and you must also calculate how willing you are to cut off your ties with home.

People who occupy these different categories may frequently drift from one to another. A small flat in Spain has, for many people, prompted, over a period of years, the move into a small catering, property or related service industry business. Those who have a holiday home may also want to use the property in Spain during retirement. However, the requirements of each category are quite different. A remote and spectacular cliffside villa which might suit a young childless couple for holidays is not going to appeal to the same people as a retirement home or somewhere to work and raise a family. Multi-purpose homes which suit families at all stages of their lives are as elusive in Spain as they are anywhere else in the world. If you intend to keep a residence in Spain over a period of decades, you should, if you intend to use it regularly, expect to change homes to meet your altered needs.

FOREIGN PROPERTY AS INVESTMENTS

One of the first questions which any potential purchaser asks of an estate agent is – what will it be worth in a few years' time? An honest estate agent will be hard pressed to give a firm answer.

In Britain, homeowners have become used to the idea that the simple possession of bricks and mortar, usually through a large mortgage, is, in itself, a guarantee of sizable investment returns within the space of a few years. Rising house prices, particularly in the south east of England, have left families with residual property values which, if they are realised, result in capital sums far beyond any which the same people might save in conventional ways.

We tend to regard this trend as the norm; in reality it is the exception. Generally speaking, property ownership on the Continent is not a way of building up large residual values through a housing market which increases in price ahead of the rate of inflation. Most Europeans move house for understandable reasons – they need extra space, they are earning more money, or they have changed jobs, for instance. Property, while a sound investment, is not an alternative to an interest-bearing bank deposit account.

This is the case in most of Spain. However, the influx of north Europeans to tourist areas has brought a degree of property speculation with it. In the next chapter which discusses the different regions of Spain, I have given a general guide to areas where financial gains have been made in the past through property, and might be made in the future. These comments can only be rough-and-ready, and you would be well advised to assume that any property in Spain will *never* give you the kind of substantial returns which could be had in England at the height of the property boom of the mid 1980s.

Of course, it is debatable whether those gains will ever be available in England again. The only thing one can say with certainty about any property market is that, in normal conditions, housing will remain a safe, if unspectacular, investment. Some people in Spain have found otherwise – with good *and* bad surprises. Areas which were unknown a decade ago may become fashionable, giving substantial profits to those who bought their homes early, for low prices. Equally, purchasers have been persuaded to pay for homes in out-of-the-way developments which have never become popular, and paid the cost. Like any property speculation, there is a gamble involved.

The safest route is to regard your home in Spain primarily as an investment in pleasure which will retain, in real terms, its financial value in the years to come and may even give you a pleasant surprise when you come to sell.

THE FACES OF SPAIN

You could spend a lifetime wandering around Spain looking for your perfect property. Inevitably, you will have to narrow down your choice before you begin to look. A breakdown of the principal areas is included in the next chapter. But within each region, there are different kinds of communities which need to be considered.

Coastal resorts

Most people buy a home in one of the popular coastal resorts, often one they were introduced to through a package holiday. Large seaside towns, such as Marbella and Benidorm, have well-established facilities for property sales, including English-speaking estate agencies and lawyers. Such places normally have a year-round foreign population, running cafés, bars and restaurants and the usual round of services one would expect back home. British builders and plumbers will advertise in the local papers offering what they hope is a more reliable service than their Spanish counterparts.

Buying into an established development in a busy resort is the easiest way into Spain. You will have little difficulty finding good professional advice, and the very popularity of the resort will normally mean that there are good air links with other countries. Most properties will be within walking distance of the resort centre, or have good public transport. This reduces the need for a private car, something which can be a burden to the owner who visits for only a few months of the year.

You should be wary on several points, however. The price of resort properties can fluctuate with the fashionability of the area. In the last decade there has been something of a swing away from the Costa Brava and Blanca towards the south. Being caught at the wrong end of such a movement will reduce the investment value of your property. There is also a degree of uncertainty about the long-term future of the conventional package holiday resort. In recent years, there has been a marked shift away from standard, two-week packaged hotel holidays. While the number of people looking for self-catering accommodation has risen steadily, the vast hotels market appears to be in decline. This has already resulted in some hotels being turned into apartment blocks, deflating property prices in the area. Fewer visitors have also meant a static local economy overall which may be reflected in empty commercial sites and some urban decay in a few areas.

Lawyers should ensure that thorough checks are made to see that, as far as possible, the property which interests you will not be affected by redevelopment schemes. These safeguards are most needed in the busy resort areas, where new roads and municipal facilities are often being planned. As a general rule, avoid all properties which overlook busy main roads. Their resale value will be low and you may safely assume that, however choked the road is today, tomorrow will be worse.

You should expect the facilities of the average resort property to be somewhat lower in quality than you would find on one of the new generation of estates, purpose built for the foreign market. Many of the cheaper apartments in the resorts are in blocks which are now 20 years old. A studio apartment can be found for under £15,000 but it is unlikely to have access to a private garden or pool, and maintenance charges may be inordinately high. If there is open space close to the property, you should assume that it is likely to be built upon, unless your lawyer can assure you firmly to the contrary.

Finally, if you are looking at an apartment property, consider the general nature of the block. Is it primarily owned by foreigners, or principally Spanish? Most important of all, do holiday companies take out block bookings of the apartments for package tours? Transient package holidaymakers can make noisy neighbours and there is precious little you can do to complain, as you can with an unruly permanent resident, English or Spanish, who is disturbing your sleep.

New estates – developments in outer resort areas

The boom in new Spanish homes is happening at the perimeter of existing resorts. The mass market development of the past has been set aside for more elegant – and more expensive – designer homes. Few of these new estates are of the tower-block variety. Most are a mixture of villas and low-rise apartments set in private gardens. The imagination of Spanish architects has been let loose on several schemes, from Nerja's well-known El Capistrano, which is designed to resemble an Andalucian village, to the oddly organic outlines of the Benalmadena marina development which owes much to the ideas of the eccentric Barcelona architect Gaudí.

This new style of holiday development offers several advantages over the old town centre blocks. Homes are secure and the estate usually well managed, often with attractive gardens and pools which may only be used by residents. The semi-rural locations afford peace and quiet but are not remote from resort facilities. However, the use of a car is likely to be essential. In general, the building standards are much higher than an earlier generation of Spanish development, with fitted kitchens, insulation and that ubiquitous utility of the Mediterranean expatriate, satellite television, already installed in many of the estates on offer.

What can go wrong?

Perhaps the commonest disappointment is the discovery that, after a few years, your hideaway estate is no longer as private as it used to be. Building in rural areas is more strictly controlled than it was, which tends to confine new estates to areas which are already developed. Solitude may be short-lived, although it is unlikely that a major estate will appear instantly on your doorstep without prior warning from your lawyer at the contracts stage.

One occasional difficulty with out-of-town developments can be impractical siting of an estate. In some parts, builders have been more keen to find spectacular views for their homes than to create estates which are realistic from such mundane points of view as access. Developments have been perched on the top of rocky outcrops or beetling slopes, linked by narrow winding roads which defy removals vans. There is at least one estate in Mallorca where items of furniture must be carried by hand several hundred feet up a steep hillside to reach the front doors of several villas.

If you have the money, there is much to be said for out-of-town developments. The more popular, like the large La Sotogrande estate west of Marbella, which is virtually a £53 million new town, are already proving to be sound investments for resale, even after only a few years. A two-bedroom flat at Sotogrande bought for £45,000 in 1985 was on the market for more than £100,000 four years later.

'Real' Spain

Some purchasers are intent on leaving behind the resorts as quickly as they can and heading out into a Spain largely unaffected by mass tourism. Beyond the main tourist areas, property prices plummet. Country homes with orange groves and vineyards can be found for the cost of a one-bedroomed apartment in Marbella. Nor are some of these rural properties unduly remote. Even in Mallorca, you can find small estates away from the coast which are relatively inexpensive, and a number of foreign buyers have picked up bargains in the countryside which lies behind the Costa del Sol, the mountains of the Alpujarra, east of Málaga and around towns such as Coín and Alhaurin El Grande in the west. Similar low-priced properties can be found by travelling further afield from most of the popular holiday destinations. Coastal areas which have not been developed for international tourism have a limited number of low-priced holiday villas and apartments, often with excellent beaches nearby.

If you want to live in 'real' Spain, you must be prepared to act like a Spaniard. This is not simply a question of buying a car and learning the language. You must understand local customs and mores, and follow them. Local people are remarkably unmoved by the arrival of foreign residents, even when their money has caused high property prices. There is little, if any, of the resentment towards outsiders seen in regions like Wales where some residents regard foreigners as unwelcome visitors whose wealth is robbing the local population of its heritage. Everyone in Spain understands that tourism and foreign visitors spell income for the whole community.

How good an investment is an out-of-the-way property? It depends how out-of-the-way it is. Any home which is difficult to reach easily from one of the main Spanish airports is unlikely to rise appreciably in value, since it will be hard to sell it to another foreign buyer. However, communications links do change. In the early 1980s it was possible to buy very inexpensive property in the area around Gibraltar. Travel was a serious problem. The border at Gibraltar was closed, and the nearest international airports were at Seville and Málaga, three hours away by car.

Since the reopening of the border, the western end of the Costa del Sol has revived and is now the most active in terms of new developments. Villas bought for £20,000 in the early 1980s may now change hands for five or six times that price. The development of smaller tourist airports, such as Almeria in the south, and Lanzarote and Fuerteventura in the Canary Islands *may* revive rural property prices.

But if your villa is in a lovely *pueblo* several hours from the nearest international airport it will never appreciate in value much beyond the rate of inflation.

SPORTS FACILITIES

Whether you are looking for a holiday home or a primary residence, sport and leisure facilities are likely to be important factors in your decision. In northern Europe, the presence of a good marina or tennis courts may be a minor priority; in Spain leisure facilities can be a key factor in determining the price and popularity of an area or development. This is not just a matter of 'wanting to be close to the sea' if you intend to go scuba diving daily – it is a question of the style of life which you want to pursue in your new home.

Sports facilities are limited in remote rural locations, but abound in virtually all the tourist areas. Tennis courts are often attached to apartment blocks; if not, you will normally be able to pay to play on a court attached to a local hotel. Virtually every modern apartment block will have a communal swimming pool, and pools are also added to almost every private villa. The absence of a pool lowers the selling price of any villa which could accommodate one; the cost of installing one of the common pools available from local specialist firms, which begin at around £7,500, should be included in your estimates of what your property will cost you in years to come.

Golf courses are common throughout Spain, several of them designed by world class golfers. The cost of membership of leading golf clubs is high, more than one would expect to pay at British clubs of similar standing. While the courses remain popular with locals, and often have a busy social side, their cost has driven away many of the package holiday golfers who find neighbouring Portugal cheaper.

The waters of tourist Spain throng with pleasure craft throughout the year and in Puerto Banus, next to Marbella, the Costa del Sol has a marina which attracts as many millionaires and jet-setters as anywhere in the south of France. The cost of moorings varies according to the fashionability and facilities of the marina. There is a steady market in resale craft of all types and sizes, often through English boat brokers. If you are looking for a boat, visit one of the large marinas where you will normally find several brokers' offices and a forest of 'For Sale' signs on the flotilla of craft at their moorings. On an average day in Palma, Mallorca, a stroll along the city waterfront might reveal a small ocean-going yacht for £15,000, a converted North Sea trawler for £50,000, and a luxury pleasure cruiser for £1 million, all moored within a few hundred yards of each other.

LEARNING SPANISH

A knowledge of Spanish is invaluable wherever you stay. In a package resort, it will help you deal with local people on a more friendly basis. In rural Spain, and even in large cities with little interest in tourism, Spanish is indispensable. Outside the tourist areas, very few people speak English, even in hotels, lawyers' offices and estate agencies.

However, learning Spanish, even a little, is more than just a matter of practicalities. The Spanish are proud people who are flattered by foreigners who have made some effort to learn their language. They are all too familiar with the north European, particularly the Briton, who assumes that his or her own language is the mother tongue of the whole world. A few words of Spanish can transform surly officials into helpful ones and ease your path through the many bureaucratic corridors which face you. Speaking Spanish will also help you get far more out of the country. When travelling you will find local people anxious to explain the sights, the best restaurants, and the ideal parking places... if you can understand them.

If you fail to learn Spanish, you will, effectively, be trapped in those areas which are accustomed to foreign tourists, and confined to the company of your fellow expatriates. This would be a great shame; many of the best experiences of modern Spain are to be found beyond the resorts and the tourist traps of the large cities. Places like Seville, which on the surface seem mere mechanical extensions of the tourist industry, take on another dimension when you are able to take part in the street life and fiestas as easily as the locals. If you intend to do business in Spain, good spoken Spanish is essential and written desirable.

There are language schools in all the main resorts which offer crash courses in Spanish. Correspondence and cassette tape courses make adequate alternatives for those away from the resorts. You may find it a good idea to enrol at night school before leaving Britain so that you have broken the ice in the subject when you arrive. There are regular classes at local authority night schools. Beware the very basic courses in Spanish, which are intended primarily as a way of enabling package holidaymakers to order food and drink, and ask for everyday items in a local language. While these may make good introductions to Spanish, they are unlikely to be sufficient for anyone spending more than a few weeks in the country, or wishing to do business.

Spanish is not a difficult language to learn, though the regional accents can sometimes cause some confusion, even for the Spanish themselves. The principal problem encountered by those newly graduated from language courses is that Spaniards, once they recognise a foreigner with a knowledge of their language, frequently relax into the machine gun rattle speech which is their norm. A polite request to speak more slowly will often bring comprehension to a stream of words which was hitherto unrecognisable.

The language which we regard as Spanish is Castillian, the tongue of Madrid and the south which, under Franco, was the only language allowed to be spoken in Spain. The native tongue of Catalonia is Catalan, and a bastardised version of it is also the local language in Mallorca. Many Spanish schools now speak both tongues and, in the relevant areas, you will find that street signs and official documents appear in the local language or in both Catalan and Castillian.

Speaking Catalan, or, in Mallorca, Mallorquin, will win you much admiration in these places, but it is of little practical use elsewhere. If offered the choice, always learn Castillian; you may be assured that all Spaniards understand Castillian, not everyone can follow Catalan.

THE ESSENTIAL CHECKLIST

Your motives:
- holiday home/second home
- retirement home – 1st or 2nd home
- emigration, to live and work as a resident

Your choices:
- coastal resort, apartment or villa
- new estate, resort perimeter
- major city, without tourist trade
- rural isolation

Considerations:
- will you have a car?
- do you need commercial facilities close by?
- wide range of shopping/dining facilities?
- do you want a small local community?
- would you prefer an expatriate community?
- will you learn Spanish?
- do you need good air links to the UK?
- leisure and sports facilities?

SPAIN
N
FRANCE
Pyrenees
Perpignan
Santanda
Bilbao
La Coruna
Oviedo
ASTURIAS
Cordillera Cantabrica
Leon
Burgos
LA RIOJA
CATALUNA
R. Mino
GALICIA
R. Ebro
R. Segre
CASTILLA Y LEON
Valladolid
Zaragoza
Barcelona
Costa Brava
Costa Dorada
R. Douro
Guadarramas
Sierra de Albarracin
Sierra de Gredos
Madrid
VALENCIA
PORTUGAL
R. Turia
Costa Azahar
BALEARIC ISLANDS
Minorca
Palma
Majorca
Ibiza
Formentera
MEDITERRANEAN SEA
EXTREMADURA
R. Tajo
La Mancha
Valencia
R. Júcar
R. Guadiana
Badajoz
Sierra Morena
Sierra Segura
Alicante
Murcia
Costa Blanca
R. Guadalquivir
ANDALUCIA
Sevilla
R. Genil
Granada
Sierra Nevada
Almeria
Costa Calida
Costa de Almeria
Malaga
Costa del Sol
Cadiz
Costa de la Luz
MOROCCO
kilometres 0 100 200 300
CANARY ISLANDS
La Palma
Sta Cruz de la Palma
La Laguna
Sta Cruz de Tenerife
Gomera
Tenerife
Hierro
kilometres 0 100
Las Palmas
Gran Canaria
Arrecife
Lanzarote
Pto del Rosario
Fuerteventura
Tarfaya
MOROCCO

2 The Regions of Spain

There is an old travel writing cliché which runs 'Ruritania is a land of many contrasts...' Well, Spain *is* a land of many contrasts, cliché or no. The prospective resident needs to think long and hard about which of its many faces he or she would like to enjoy, inland or coastal, historic or modern.

The great majority of property sales in Spain take place in three areas most familiar to the north European visitor – the Costa del Sol, the Balearics, and the Canary Islands. These regions are profiled in some detail here, with shorter descriptions of less popular, though equally attractive, areas.

THE COSTA DEL SOL

The Mediterranean coastline of Andalucia – the Costa del Sol – is often the first area to spring to mind when people think of a home in Spain. The region has an unrivalled selection of new, timeshare and resale properties in locations which vary from busy seaside resorts to quiet, private hillside developments. If you want a home which is easy to reach and has a good chance of appreciating in value over the rate of inflation, then the Costa del Sol must be your first choice. Communications are excellent – Málaga airport is one of the busiest in Spain, with regular schedule and charter flights from Europe. In the height of summer, the very popularity of Málaga can result in some flight delays, particularly from southern England. Seasoned travellers will choose to shop around and book on scheduled rather than the more common charter flights of the package tour companies.

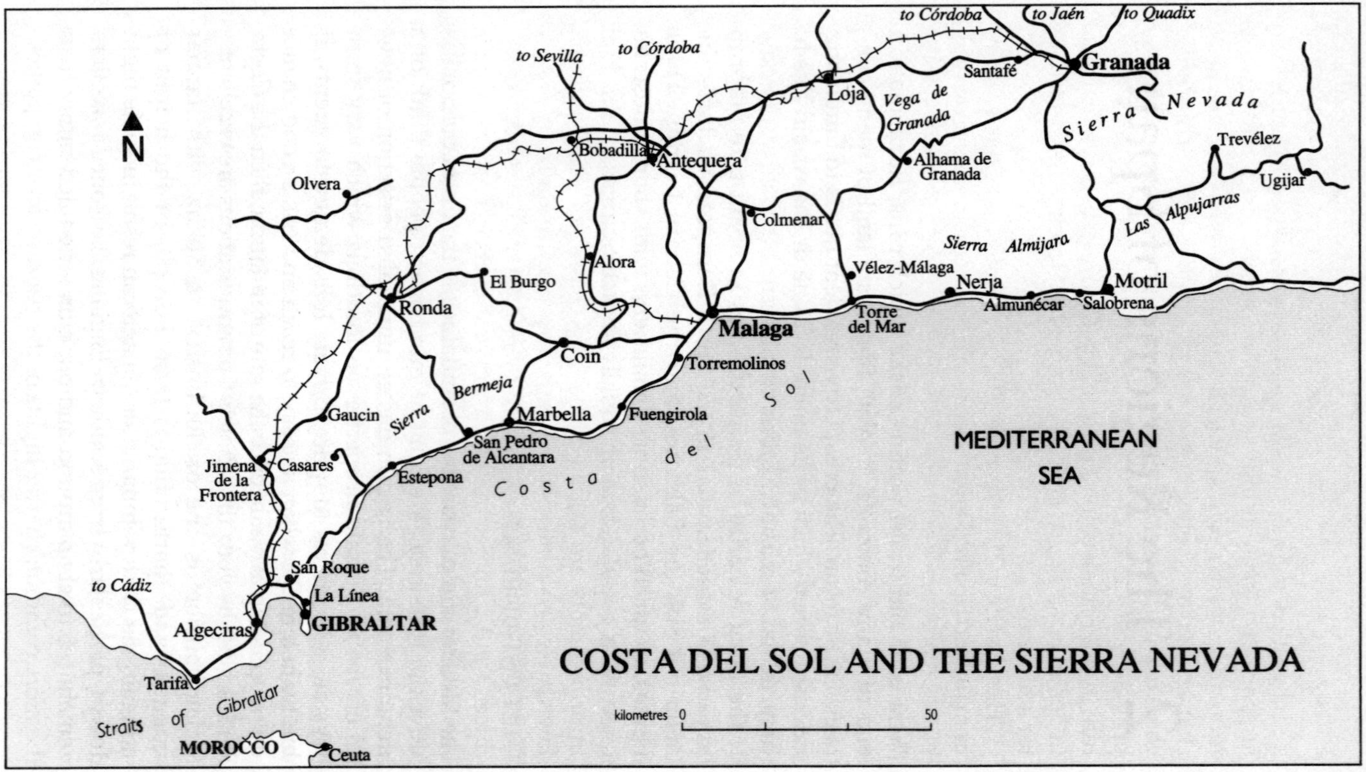
COSTA DEL SOL AND THE SIERRA NEVADA
N
to Sevilla
to Córdoba
to Córdoba
to Jaén
to Quadix
Granada
Santafé
Loja
Vega de Granada
Sierra Nevada
Trevélez
Ugijar
Las Alpujarras
Alhama de Granada
Bobadilla
Antequera
Olvera
Colmenar
Sierra Almijara
Alora
Vélez-Málaga
Nerja
Motril
El Burgo
Ronda
Malaga
Torre del Mar
Almunécar
Salobrena
Coin
Torremolinos
Sierra Bermeja
Gaucin
Marbella
Fuengirola
Costa del Sol
San Pedro de Alcantara
MEDITERRANEAN SEA
Jimena de la Frontera
Casares
Estepona
San Roque
to Cádiz
La Línea
Algeciras
GIBRALTAR
Tarifa
Straits of Gibraltar
MOROCCO
Ceuta
kilometres 0 50

Scheduled flights always receive precedence in congested airspace and, even in high season, may only cost a few pounds more than charter equivalents, a small price to pay for a reduced chance of delays, better in-flight service and less time-consuming checking-in facilities. Charter and scheduled flights to Gibraltar provide ready access to the western end of the Costa del Sol. Car hire in the British colony is somewhat more expensive than that in Spain, however, so cross the border to Algeciras before paying for a hire car.

The climate of the Costa del Sol is as attractive as one will find in mainland Spain. The summers are hot, occasionally scorching, but sea breezes normally dull the edge of the hottest days. Winters are mild with occasional rain, but there are often periods of sunny, warm weather in November and February.

All major towns have English-speaking – and frequently English-owned – estate agencies, and it is not hard to find English-speaking professional advisers. The principal objection to the Costa del Sol is the very scale of the development. There is already little open space left between Málaga and Marbella. The notorious main road, the N340 *Carretera del Muerte* (Highway of Death), so called because of its numerous fatal accidents, cannot cope with the volume of traffic imposed upon it, although improvements are taking place. The centres of Torremolinos, Fuengirola and Marbella are choked with traffic daily.

Stricter controls on building development have been introduced, and prevent the construction of large, high-rise apartment blocks close to the coast. However, upmarket estate developments seem welcome. It seems inevitable that, within a decade or so, the coastline will be continuous development as far as Estepona. Beyond Estepona lies unattractive, scrubby countryside with a few developments. The landscape improves briefly before Gibraltar, and it is here that two of the largest new developments have been built, Sotogrande and La Duquesa, both stylish, well equipped with facilities and expensive.

Until recently, the coastline east of Málaga was largely ignored by the tourist trade, but this is rapidly changing. There is a great deal of development around the three principal coastal towns of Nerja, Almuñécar, and Salobreña. Tourist facilities remain relatively simple compared with those of Marbella and

Torremolinos, but there is every indication that the east will one day catch up with the west.

Behind much of the coast lies interesting and attractive mountainous countryside, with a few rural developments for tourists. Individual country properties remain reasonably priced, although a decade ago they could be bought for a song. The towns of Coín and Alhaurin El Grande are worthy of investigation to the west; to the east lies the mountain region of the Alpujarra. The latter is an area which tourist authorities believe will become an important tourist centre in years to come. The small mountain towns of Orgiva, Lanjarón, Bubion and Capileira are largely unspoilt, with only a few small hotels and a handful of restaurants. The pace of life is extremely slow, and properties inexpensive, if increasing in price as the word spreads. The coast and Málaga airport are only an hour or so away; for a home which is well away from the tourist bustle but still in touch with civilisation, the Alpujarra may be a good bet. However, you will have to deal with largely Spanish-speaking estate agents, and probably need to track down properties personally.

Torremolinos

Less than 40 years ago, Torremolinos was a line of fishermen's cottages and a single roadside hotel. An aerial picture of the time still adorns a couple of cafés in the town to remind locals of what their home once was. Today, the cottages remain, most of them turned into popular fish restaurants, and around them stands a mass of hotels, apartment blocks and villas that can, at a push, accommodate around 250,000 people. On its eastern side, towards Málaga, lies the new resort town with the long beach of Playa del Bajondillo, a selection of apartment blocks, and the usual range of resort nightclubs, discos, bars and restaurants. To the west lies the original village, La Carihuela, and the quiet residential area of Montemar.

The line of seafront development now reaches neighbouring Benalmadena, similar in style to eastern Torremolinos with a swish new marina complex with several large apartment developments. The centre of town is almost completely commercial; only a few apartment blocks remain and they are not popular.

The biggest single factor determining price in Torremolinos is proximity to the main road which cuts through the centre of town. Properties which lie on the beach side of the road carry higher values than those behind it. The few apartment blocks which lie on the road itself are likely to prove extremely difficult to resell.

Prices in Torremolinos are relatively low, in spite of the town's many amenities – the restaurants are as good as any on the coast and the beaches reasonable, and Málaga airport is only ten minutes away by car. This is partly because of the town's rather unearned reputation as a lowlife resort, and also because for many years it was a suburb of Málaga, not a *pueblo* in its own right. Torremolinos has now been given its 'independence', which allows the town to retain local taxes and spend them on public amenities. A considerable and much-needed clean-up campaign has begun to improve local drainage and roads. One of the most impressive results will be the creation of a beach-front, traffic-free promenade from Benalmadena to the eastern perimeter of the town, some three miles distant, a task which is under way at the time of writing.

Properties in La Carihuela, Montemar and the east of town have been somewhat blighted by the lack of public works in recent years, and are consequently underpriced when compared with neighbouring Fuengirola and Marbella. Torremolinos may not sound chic, but it could offer an inexpensive first entry into the Spanish property chain for someone who makes a wise buy in one of the quieter residential areas.

Fuengirola

The local expatriates of Torremolinos joke that Fuengirola is the place they'll move to when they grow old. It is a distinctly more sedate town than its eastern neighbour – *if* your home is well away from the choked and chaotic main road. Fuengirola is very popular with Britons of a certain age who form a lively, expatriate community replete with bridge clubs, friendly organisations and less formal social circles. The principal residential area is Los Boliches, to the east of the town, which has a wide range of apartments at reasonable prices. Fuengirola has been affected for some time by an inadequate traffic system which causes frequent long queues. Properties overlooking the busy roads are, naturally, unpopular and will be difficult to resell.

The village of Mijas, on hills overlooking Fuengirola, is the site of several upmarket villa and apartment developments which are rapidly becoming smart Costa del Sol addresses, and attract commensurately high purchase prices. The firmest prices are for properties in Mijas, or close by, and for apartments on the Fuengirola waterfront. The character of Mijas, which was once a modest, if attractive, Andalucian hill village, is becoming ever more cosmopolitan as the years pass, and care should be taken here to check up on the likelihood of nearby developments.

Marbella

An untold number of film stars, millionaires, television celebrities and a few rich, exiled criminals number themselves among the residents of Marbella. In its way, the town is as *chic* as St Tropez or Biarritz, stocked with fine, expensive shops and restaurants, with a good supply of beaches, golf courses and one smart marina nearby. Marbella is the most fashionable address on the Costa del Sol, but one is sometimes surprised by the ease with which tourist developments several miles distant claim the designer label with little to recommend them.

The town of Marbella is compact, if not downright overcrowded, and lies alongside the busy coastal road. There is an attractive old town set back from the road but little by the waterfront dates back to pre-1955 when Marbella was still just another poor Andalucian fishing village. Virtually all the fashionable addresses lie in the developments which line the coastal road for several miles on either side of the town itself. Some are beautifully designed and guaranteed investments for the future; others, particularly among the older developments, are hasty attempts to snatch the tourist dollar or pound as soon as it is proffered.

All are custom-made tourist estates which make little or no pretence about their true character. It is impossible to live in Marbella – or, more accurately, to live in one of its suburbs – without acknowledging that you are in the centre of tourist Spain's most glittering focal point. Marbella has a round of cocktail parties, balls and social events which can match those of

London or New York with ease, which is all very well if you have the introductions and the money to keep up with the neighbours.

The smartest piece of coastline is the stretch west of Marbella to the custom-made port of Puerto Banus, which includes developments such as Nueva Andalucia and the original Marbella Club which introduced tourism to the area. Puerto Banus itself has proved a popular and worthwhile investment for anyone who originally took one of the first apartments to be offered at the upmarket marina which now moors pleasure boats for the Middle East sheiks, Hollywood moguls and European businessmen who have the cash. If your eye is set on this side of Marbella, then expect to pay serious money. Elsewhere, particularly in the line of developments between Marbella and Fuengirola, prices are lower but the very tag of 'Marbella' always adds a few thousand pounds to the most modest of estate apartments.

San Pedro de Alcántara and Estepona

These two small towns west of Marbella escaped the effects of tourist development for many years and, in character, remain somewhat quiet and unsophisticated compared with their eastern neighbour. It is debatable how long this sense of detachment can last; the eyes of the building industry seem to have fixed themselves upon the empty acres around San Pedro and Estepona and scores of developments are now under way.

All the indications are that both towns will see the lion's share of new, small estate development on the Costa del Sol over the next five years. Most developers are constructing upmarket apartment and villa estates which sell for relatively high prices, and there is a genuine belief that, within a decade, both towns will match Marbella for the quality and selling price of their homes. Both, much to their chagrin, are sometimes called 'Marbella West', an indication, were one needed, of how they are seen by property marketing men.

However, both San Pedro and Estepona are rather gauche communities at the moment, small town Spain with most of the disadvantages and few of the good points. Nor are they particularly well placed for communications to the airport – the choked roads of Marbella and Fuengirola lie between here and Málaga, while Gibraltar is still an hour or so away. The conviction of the property industry that 'Marbella West' is where the future lies for building in the Costa del Sol *may* be proven true in years to come. But, for the moment, property purchases here should be researched particularly well, and I would recommend that you take a good look at existing facilities in San Pedro and Estepona to find if they are to your taste.

Sotogrande and the road to Gibraltar

Beyond Estepona, travelling west, the countryside is rather tedious for most of the journey to Gibraltar. However, there are a few developments, and two are among the largest in Spain. La Duquesa is centred around a new marina and lies in a frankly dull landscape, though this has not dissuaded residents attracted by the golf, tennis, and water sports. Sotogrande, covering some 4,400 acres, is a new tourist town, with two golf courses and many other sports facilities, situated in more attractive hill country 20 minutes by car from Gibraltar. Both are tourist developments pure and simple, but have excellent facilities and, from present indications, offer reasonable investment opportunities. Gibraltar is the natural airport for this part of the Costa del Sol. Travel by car east to Málaga is time-consuming and occasionally difficult. At the moment, La Duquesa and Sotogrande are for people who are seeking to escape the pressures of modern life, and do not want to be actively involved in the social and business whirl of the Costa del Sol.

Nerja, Almuñécar and Salobreña

The coastline east of Málaga is more rocky and undeveloped than its western counterpart. A number of new estates have been built in the last few years, and there is particularly intense development at Nerja and Almuñécar. Nerja is essentially a villa and apartments town, with a burgeoning building trade set around the original old town with its Balcon de Europa, a small headland from which there are views of the coast. A few years ago, Nerja had the reputation of being one of the coast's secret hideaways; today the secret is no more. Its best-known complex is El Capistrano, a new Spanish village built in Andalucian style on the edge of town, and there is a flourishing market in resales of apartments and villas in older developments. The small inland village of Frigiliana performs much the same function for Nerja as Mijas does for Fuengirola; it is a small, quite charming community with a growing number of private villas for foreigners. Nerja has an active, English-speaking resident community, with social organisations which arrange visits to other parts of Andalucia. The facilities for foreign residents are generally excellent, but the original town is hard pressed to meet the scale of development now taking place. Traffic jams are ever present, and the centre, near the Balcon, becomes extremely crowded for most of the summer.

Almuñécar and Salobreña are more modest Spanish resort towns which are now making a concerted attempt to capture the foreign tourist trade. The developments west of Almuñécar, around the Punte de la Mona and at the new harbour of Marina del Este, offer beautiful locations and some guarantees of privacy and safeguards against over-development. In some ways, they are more attractive than the lines of new estates crowding the Málaga-Sotogrande strip to the west, if peace and quiet is what you are looking for and you do not need a great choice of local facilities. Cheaper apartments and villas are widely available in both Almuñécar and Salobreña. The towns are similar in character, modest, essentially Spanish and with reasonable beaches nearby. You should not expect to meet a large expatriate community or a wealth of foreign restaurants here, but this may change in years to come as the area becomes more popular. Winters, even in Nerja, are very quiet indeed.

Nerja is the only town east of Málaga which could be said to be fashionable. Prices can be fairly stiff here for the best properties, but they are still less than one would pay in most of the new developments to the west. Bargain hunters can pick up simple apartments very cheaply in Almuñécar and Salobreña, and the cost of units in the more upmarket developments remains reasonable. Beware of properties east of Salobreña where beaches may be affected by industrial pollution from the nearby, unlovely port of Motril.

It is possible that this stretch of coastline will one day become as popular as the western Costa del Sol, giving those who get in early a healthy profit on their property investment. This is by no means a certainty, however, whatever the estate agents say. Parts of the coastline are lovely, but it is a less practical area than the west, particularly for those who want to make frequent, short visits. Travel to the international airport is considerably more difficult, and entails driving through the centre of Málaga.

A few foreigners have bought property in the regional capital itself, a busy port city of much bustle and some rough edges. There is a pleasant beachside district with apartments and houses at the foot of the Gibralfaro hill and some attractive suburbs but they are almost exclusively the preserve of locals.

THE BALEARIC ISLANDS

Most visitors to Spain will know one of the Balearic Islands, usually the largest and most popular, Mallorca. The four principal islands of the group are Mallorca, Ibiza, Menorca and Formentera. They are situated in the northern Mediterranean, off the coast of Catalonia, and look to Barcelona as their regional capital. Timeshare is relatively rare in the Balearics, but there is an extremely active conventional property market dealing in a wide range of studios, apartments and villas.

The Balearics' weather system offers hot summers with the occasional violent Mediterranean storm, normally in September. Winters can be pleasant but distinctly chilly, and log fires are common in rural homes on high ground.

Mallorca

The customary image of Mallorca – as a busy beach resort lined with concrete tower blocks – is quite false. Modern, man-made resorts account for a small proportion of the island's coastline. Mallorca can offer standard beachside homes of the highest quality and remote mountain cottages in villages where the everyday language is the Catalan dialect of Mallorquin.

The bulk of new development is along the coastline west of the capital, Palma, through resorts such as Santa Ponsa and Paguera to Puerto de Andraitx. There is also widescale development along the Bay of Alcudia, and in Puerto de Pollensa.

New, small villa communities are appearing along the length of the east coast. Most modern Mallorcan development is well-designed, spacious, peaceful... and expensive. Some of the better developments close to Palma can happily ask £100,000 for an apartment. However, there is a stock of cheaper, older-style apartments in resort areas such as Illetas, Paguera, Santa Ponsa, Palma Nova and Magalluf.

It is still possible to pick up low-priced rural houses, particularly ones which require renovation. Some Mallorcan hill villages, in the north west, such as Puigpunyent, Fornalutx and Banyalbufar, are now fashionable. Properties are hard to find and fetch reasonably high prices. In other, less attractive locations, ordinary country homes can be found from £30,000. In general, property in Mallorca can prove a reasonable investment, provided that you have chosen wisely.

Palma itself, a busy commercial city with an attractive waterfront, is increasingly popular for holiday apartments. Prices for flats on the Paseo Marítimo, the broad sweep of road which runs along the bay, have hardened considerably in recent years with the announcement of plans to build a bypass around the city. The new road should relieve the pressure of traffic on the Paseo. There are several new high-priced blocks overlooking the bay, and many cheaper flats available in the somewhat down-at-heel suburb of Terreno which lies behind the Paseo to the west. Palma is on the way to becoming a fashionable European city, with high-priced fashion shops, a sophisticated nightlife, and a busy social scene. It could well prove a sound investment for the property buyer. The city has extensive marina facilities for craft of all sizes.

Mallorca has around 30,000 English-speaking full-time residents and many more part-time visitors. The island has a busy social round of organisations, principally for the middle-aged, with dining clubs and friendly organisations competing for members. The focal point for much of the social life of the island is the English language daily paper, the *Daily Bulletin*, which has regular columns on activities in the principal residential areas. Estate agents advertise their wares regularly in the *Bulletin*, and small ads also offer properties privately, as well as furniture, cars and maintenance services.

Palma is extremely easy to reach from northern Europe. The airport receives charter and scheduled flights daily throughout the year. The centre of the city is only a ten-minute drive away. An eight-hour ferry to Barcelona is popular with residents who wish to take their cars to Europe. Ferries also link Mallorca with Ibiza and Menorca.

Ibiza, Menorca and Formentera

Ibiza made its name as a Mediterranean paradise for hippies. Much of the underground sub-culture has now disappeared, but the island remains somewhat aloof from its neighbours. Several rock stars have Ibizan homes.

The three main tourist areas are the town of Ibiza itself, which is heavily developed, the beach resort of San Antonio Abad, and the quieter town of Santa Eulalia. Properties can also be found in small coastal developments, often of high quality. The inland communities are generally small and have few facilities; they attract some foreign buyers, usually those interested in living like the locals. Summers are hectic and hot; in winter most facilities are closed.

Like Ibiza, Menorca is primarily a summer resort, and even then it is much quieter than its two neighbours. Menorca is green, peaceful and relatively unspoilt. The principal resort areas are around Ciudadela, Binibeca and Arenal d'En Castell, but villas and traditional farmhouses for sale can be found throughout the island.

The island of Formentera, which is reached by ferry from Ibiza town, is quiet and largely unspoilt. Most facilities close during the winter. A small number of apartments and villas are foreign-owned by people seeking out-of-the-way summer breaks. The principal resorts, all of them very small, are Es Calo, Es Pujols, La Sabina, Playa de Mitjorn, San Fernando and San Francisco Javier.

There are regular charter and scheduled flights to Ibiza and Menorca during the summer, but they are few and far between during the winter.

THE CANARY ISLANDS

Situated off the coast of North Africa, the Canary Islands are closer to the Equator than is Bermuda. There are seven inhabited islands scattered over 300 miles, the principal ones of interest to the tourist being Tenerife, Gran Canaria, Lanzarote and Fuerteventura. They fall into two Spanish provinces, one run from Tenerife, the second from Gran Canaria. Warm winters and the promise of sun in February and November bring many thousands of visitors from northern Europe, and their numbers increase yearly. Timeshare and villa developments are popular on all three principal islands, and there have been sizable financial gains for those who have bought wisely in resorts which have later become sought after.

The Canary Islands have belonged to Spain since the 15th century but, until the advent of mass tourism, were colonial backwaters principally used as ports of call for craft crossing the Atlantic. While the scenery is frequently spectacular, compared with the mainland there is little in the way of culture or attractive old towns. The cuisine of the islands is limited and some items are expensive, since most commodities have to be imported. Most properties for sale or timeshare are in custom-built tourist resorts, occasionally sited around an original fishing village.

In general, the standard of accommodation is high, and, since the region was developed at a later date than mainland Spain, there are more 'designer developments'. This naturally means that most holiday homes in the Canaries are in tourist areas, pure and simple. Those in the country, or villages and small towns, are likely to be even more remote than similar properties on mainland Spain.

Lotus-eating pure and simple is the staple fare of the Canaries, though the character of each island is very individually stamped. Weather is the key to everything, and the ardent Canaries-lover is often more than happy to indulge in a spot of self-deception on this subject.

Winters on any of the islands are, it is true, invariably hotter and drier than one might reasonably expect anywhere in England. They are *not* guaranteed sun and heat all winter long, however, and at times the dark months of December and

January can be rather grim. The principal problem at this time of year stems from easterly winds which rise in the Sahara and deposit sand and dust everywhere. During these periods, the famed Canary beaches become unusable. Nor is it uncommon to experience days of grey, warm weather with leaden skies. You will still get a suntan in these conditions – the ultra violet works its way through the cloud – but one may soon learn that there is little to do in the Canaries when the sun doesn't shine. Timeshare purchasers should be particularly careful about the timing of their particular weeks.

The best times to visit are the spring and autumn when the climate is normally reliably warm and dry and all facilities are open and working. All islands are less busy during the summer when daytime temperatures may reach the 100°s, but in many ways the Canaries are a year-round destination; their low season is never as sleepy as January on the Costa del Sol.

There are a number of specialist watersport organisations for windsurfing, waterskiing, diving and sailing. The Canaries are a favourite port of call for yachtsmen crossing the Atlantic. There are golf courses on Tenerife, Gran Canaria and Lanzarote, and tennis courts in all the main resorts. Horseriding facilities and hunting trips are available on the main islands.

In general, property prices are realistic and have fluctuated little in recent years. The additional travelling time to the Canaries is a disincentive for the casual traveller. A flying time of more than four hours from England discourages people who want a second home for short breaks. There are good, busy airports on Tenerife and Gran Canaria. Those for Lanzarote and Fuerteventura do receive flights from Britain but less frequently. There are frequent inter-island flights though visitors with foreign homes rarely travel much from the island of their choice. The islands are also served by regular ferries from the major Spanish ports which can take up to a week depending on the route they take.

Tenerife

The largest island, covering 1,231 square miles, Tenerife is effectively divided into two regions by Mount Teide. The north is damp and humid and less popular with visitors; the south, dry and hot is the site of most resorts. It is perfectly possible to have a downpour of torrential rain in the north while bathers lie under clear blue skies on a southern beach. The principal airport, the Reina Sofia, is in the south. There are regular ferries from the Spanish mainland, and inter-island services.

The oldest tourist resort on the island is Puerto de la Cruz in the north, a hectic round of hotels, apartment blocks, bars, restaurants and night clubs. In the south, the boom town is Playa de las Americas which is growing rapidly and will probably become one of the island's dominant resorts. There are quieter spots in the south, however, such as Los Cristianos, purpose built for the tourist trade. One problem which can be experienced in the newer resorts is isolation. Some on the south coast are a considerable distance from established towns, and are mainly aimed at the inveterate sun-lover. Facilities such as restaurants and shops can be limited.

Gran Canaria

Although the third largest island in the group, Gran Canaria has the biggest city of the Canaries – Las Palmas, a hectic port of some 350,000 people with a picturesque old quarter. A small part of the city is set beside the beach of Playa de las Canteras, with hotels and apartments overlooking the sea. But most tourists find modern Las Palmas too busy for comfort and head out to the resorts in the south of the island.

Virtually all tourist development runs from San Agustin to Maspalomas, past the resort of Playa del Inglés. Apartment blocks, hotels and villas line the coast, but the beaches are among the best to be found in the Canaries, and the facilities are better than one will find in some of the newer, speculative developments elsewhere.

Gran Canaria does not suffer from the split climate of Tenerife. There are regular charter flights to the island, and many international carriers use Las Palmas airport as a stopover, providing good links to destinations across the Atlantic for those who require them.

Inland Gran Canaria has a great variety of scenery, from arid desert areas to lush banana plantations. There are some charming rural areas, with the occasional quite reasonably priced country house coming on to the market at odd intervals.

Lanzarote

The most curious, and most recently developed, of all the Canary Islands, Lanzarote has, in the space of a decade, become something of a boom industry. The main town of Arrecife is a fishing and industrial port of little interest, but there has been widespread development to the south, and more recently, to the north, most of it restrained and low key. There are some fine villas and apartments in Lanzarote, and some hefty profits have been pocketed by those who were smart enough to buy into the fledgling resorts when they were being created in the late 1970s.

The main resort is Puerto del Carmen, which now sprawls, quite tastefully, along the southern coast in a line of quiet villas and low-rise hotels. Other developments are under way elsewhere in the island, but none has been as successful as Puerto del Carmen, nor seem likely to emulate its achievements in the near future. Prices are occasionally inflated and, in newer developments, care should be taken to ensure that the purchaser understands precisely what is going to be built around him. Cases of new villas straying into spare parcels of land between existing homes and the sea are not uncommon, and the offending construction may well be built by the selfsame developer who promised a clear line of sight to the beach. It is doubtful whether the gains of a few years ago can still be made. The island is now well established on the package holiday market.

Lanzarote's popularity must be partly due to its cult status among holidaymakers and a reputation as a fine winter sports destination for tennis, swimming and windsurfing enthusiasts. To be frank, the leisure facilities on the island, while good, are really little different from those to be found elsewhere. Lanzarote's real asset is that it was developed after the mass package boom had faded, and has consequently escaped the worst excesses of Spanish resort development.

The island is, for the most part, distinctly ugly. Great areas are swathes of volcanic rock which are much used by feature film directors seeking locations for scenes of the moon. The beaches are reasonable, however, and the atmosphere distinctly laid back. A somewhat eccentric though much revered local architect, César Manrique, has inspired a certain style of building design on the island which may remind the unforewarned visitor of a slightly warped childhood Lego set. The island airport has been transformed out of all recognition in a decade and now receives scheduled and charter flights throughout the year.

Fuerteventura, Gomera, La Palma and El Hierro

Given Lanzarote's conversion from poor, ugly duckling to fashionable, chic resort, can the same be expected of the remaining Canary Islands? Certainly some developers believe so, and the sound of construction work can now be heard along beaches which have yet to see their first bottle of Ambre Solaire. The idea of a new affluence spreading to the rest of the Canary Islands should be treated with a degree of caution. The very isolation of the islands places limitations on the number of visitors which they are likely to attract each year, and there is no reason to expect development on the scale of that seen in the southern Spanish mainland.

Fuerteventura is the main target set in the developers' sights for the moment. Once accessible only by boat from Lanzarote, it now has a new airport and occasional charter flights from the UK. The beaches are excellent and normally utterly secluded. The largest town is the capital of Puerto del Rosario, which has a state hotel, a parador, close by, and tourist developments have been built to the north and south. If Fuerteventura is to catch up with Lanzarote, it has a very long way to go. Any villa or apartment for sale here cannot command a high price at the moment, and is unlikely to do so for several years to come... if ever. But then many people said the same about Lanzarote a decade ago, and they have been proved spectacularly wrong.

The remaining inhabited islands of the group, Gomera, La Palma and El Hierro, must be reached by local boat or flight. From the point of view of the prospective property purchaser, they are strictly for those who genuinely want to escape from it all, though there are signs that Gomera, at least, will attract regular tourist trade. The island can only be reached by boat from Tenerife and there are, at the time of writing, no tourist developments for sale, though property may be bought privately. Day visitors apart, you will rarely hear a foreign voice, and facilities of all kinds are simple. The landscape is a rugged mix of volcanic stone and wild countryside, roughly cultivated by the local farmers, the beaches are variable in quality and often hard to reach but almost always deserted.

THE COSTA BRAVA

The 'Wild Coast' of the Mediterranean runs from the border with France the length of the province of Gerona. It has been very popular with foreign property owners since the earliest days of mass tourism to Spain. There are frequent charter and schedule flights to Gerona's airport, and this is the easiest developed area of Spain to reach by private car, driving south through France via Perpignan. The coastline is rocky, with many coves and inlets. Charming, picturesque areas remain in the face of overdevelopment in some parts.

In recent years, the Costa Brava has been overshadowed, like the rest of mainland Spain, by the shift in mass development to the Costa del Sol. This has softened prices somewhat, which is fine for the buyer but disappointing when you come to sell. Nevertheless, many north Europeans live happily, part and full time, along the coast, forming an active expatriate community. It is principally an area of villa developments; there is little timeshare on offer.

While it may suit you to discover an area which is not being overdeveloped, you should beware of unfinished *urbanizaciónes* which may never be completed, and the centres of established resorts which may be affected by the disappointing level of package holiday trade in recent years. Established private villas in rural locations are often reasonably priced and may afford many years of pleasure... if you can accept that there will probably be no pleasant surprise when you finally come to sell, and can live with somewhat limited local facilities. While one might happily retire in seclusion, it might be hard to run a business here. Gerona is a busy local capital, but for international facilities one must look south to Barcelona, two hours drive from the northern part of the coast.

The resorts of Rosas, with its large marina, Blanes, Lloret de Mar, Tossa de Mar and Estartit embrace a wide range of Spanish coastal development styles, from the dull breeze block apartments of 20 years ago to more modern, stylish villa estates. Any of these would make a good base for exploring smaller villages on the coast and inland. The most fashionable address on the Costa Brava is Cadaqués, once the favourite haunt of European artists, led by the late Salvador Dalí. Property prices here are among the highest on the coast.

Summers are hot and busy, winters cooler than the south but quiet. Many resort facilities close during the off season. There are two golf courses and organisations which run riding, hanggliding, parachuting, flying, diving, walking and cycling clubs. The Costa Brava is part of Catalonia so most local people will speak Catalan first and Castillian second. Road signs and maps may use either or both languages.

THE COSTA BLANCA

The 'White Coast' runs from the Gulf of Valencia to the Gulf of Mazarron. Most tourist developments are in the north and range from dull, 20-year-old apartment blocks and estate villas to more attractive modern developments some of which rival anything on the Costa del Sol. Timeshare is nowhere near as popular as it is on the Costa del Sol. The most famous town is Benidorm, a byword for a style of package holiday in Spain which is rapidly becoming out of date. Many potential purchasers of villas and apartments look to smaller, quieter coastal towns such as Denia, with a population of 22,000, Jávea (11,000), Calpe (9,000) and Altea (11,000). The capital of the coast is the attractive town of Alicante which is served by regular charter and schedule flights from northern Europe.

The coast is divided into two distinct regions. The north is backed by the mountains of the Sierra de Aitana, the south is level sand and salt flats. There are several attractive and interesting inland towns to the north, both in the mountains and on the route towards La Mancha.

There are fine beaches along the length of the coast, golf courses at Alicante, Altea, Calpe and Torrevieja, and pleasure boat facilities in most resort areas. The climate is hot and dry during the summer, and mild in winter. The Costa Blanca is very much a summer area for tourism, however, and facilities are limited once the package holiday masses have departed.

Like the Costa Brava, the area has failed to match the Costa del Sol in the pace of its development in recent years, though there are signs that this may be changing for the better. This has both the pros and cons outlined earlier – relatively static prices, some unfinished development, and limited international facilities. There is a large resident foreign community on the coast, nevertheless, and Calpe is the home of the Foreign Property Owners' Institute (see p. 67) which can offer advice to members about property issues.

'REAL' SPAIN

The remaining regions of Spain are either little developed or are principally used by domestic tourists. Some have small areas which have become popular with foreign home buyers. These brief pen portraits can do scant justice to places which are among the most interesting in Spain. Property prices in all are lower than those found in tourist areas, but, except in the few established resort towns, you will usually need to speak Spanish to live there and certainly have the services of a translator during purchase negotiations, in order to deal with agents who have little experience of dealing with foreigners.

THE COSTA DE ALMERIA

Almeria lies to the east of the Costa del Sol, a hot, largely uninhabited province which is mainly interested in fruit and vegetable growing. In the early 1970s, tourists were first attracted to the area by the enterprising mayor of a small town of Mojácar, east of the provincial capital, Almeria. Mojácar is a friendly hill town of Moorish character, with a small community of foreign-owned villas and a few hotels. A beach resort has been developed two miles away, and there are equally modest resort facilities in Almeria itself and on the coast at Roquetas de Mar.

The area was opened up to the UK tourist by the tour company Horizon, which owns two of Mojácar's hotels and pioneered charter flights into Almeria airport. The area has not expanded greatly in recent years, and charter flights remain relatively scarce and expensive, particularly in winter. The area is a four-hour drive from Málaga or Alicante airports.

Almeria's charms are modest and leisurely. The beaches are good, and the climate superb. The area claims milder and hotter winters than any other part of Spain, and a few residents stay on for the very quiet winter months. There is nothing of cultural interest nearby, and the atmosphere is very much that of provincial Spain. Golf courses have been built at Mojácar, Almeria and Roquetas de Mar but marine facilities are somewhat mundane compared with the more developed areas. There is little rental property or timeshare.

The area has made some impact on middle to upmarket home buyers from Britain, and the slow pace of development has been reflected in some relatively high building standards. While villa prices in Mojácar remain quite high, more modest apartments can be found on the coast. It remains doubtful whether Almeria airport will ever attract large numbers of international flights, so the area is unlikely to rise greatly in value in the years to come. Nevertheless, it does offer solitude with, in some areas, small resident English-speaking communities.

The region has one of the lowest rates of rainfall in Spain. Tourist and agricultural development has already claimed a large share of existing water supplies, and there is no ready source to meet the increased demand. Shortages can be severe in summer, and emergency supplies delivered by tanker an unexpected burden. Always ask about the water supply situation before proceeding with a purchase.

THE COSTA AZAHAR

This is the coastline running north from Valencia, through rich farm land of orange groves – 'azahar' means orange blossom – and rice fields, with a continuous line of mountains behind. It is the home of the ubiquitous Spanish dish, paella and, in summer resorts, you will find the occasional paella cooking contest. There are scheduled and some charter flights into Valencia.

The coast is divided into two regions, Valencia and Castellon de la Plana. The walled town of Peñíscola, to the north, is, perhaps, the resort best known to foreign tourists, but there are small seaside towns running the length of the coast, most with good beaches and inexpensive properties. Most tourists and property owners are Spanish, often in purpose-built estates. Leisure facilities are limited but the restaurants and shopping scene is excellent.

THE COSTA CALIDA

Few foreign visitors venture into the province of Murcia, between Alicante and Almeria, but the area has several resorts popular with Spanish tourists, and the inland towns of Murcia and Lorca are interesting. The main town of the coast, Cartagena, combines the role of tourist resort with that of industrial port.

The Mar Menor, a saltwater lagoon, offers wildfowling, watersports, golf and horseriding. Property prices, usually for a range of modest villas, are low and likely to remain so, but the beaches are as good as many better known areas. Alicante is the most convenient airport, about a 90 minute drive from Cartagena. The climate is almost as dependable as that of Almeria.

THE COSTA DORADA

Barcelona lays claim to the northern part of the Costa Dorada as its own private strip of the Mediterranean. Given the interest in this most fascinating of cities, and the 1992 Olympic Games there, many more visitors will discover the delightful seaside towns of the area. The southern half falls in the province of Tarragona, and is largely used by residents of that city.

Property prices which are now modest will probably rise over the next few years in the north. Most accommodation on the market consists of modern villas or apartments in resort areas, but more interesting rural properties can be found by those willing to look for them. Whether the price rises will be maintained is a matter of pure speculation, but there is no denying the charms of some parts of this north eastern coastline. There are frequent scheduled flights to Barcelona's international airport, and Reus, near Tarragona, is a popular charter flight destination. The coast is reached conveniently by car from southern France.

The pleasant resort town of Sitges, south of Barcelona, is already familiar with foreign tourists, as is Salou in Tarragona. There remains a string of smaller resorts to be explored. This is the heart of Catalonia, famous for good food and wine and a cultural sophistication which is not found in the south. Barcelona regards itself as one of the most important cultural cities in Europe, not without reason. Summers are more temperate than the south, and winters have their chilly moments, but the climate is generally pleasant. There is a wide range of sporting facilities including golf and many miles of excellent beach though those near Barcelona suffer from pollution.

THE COSTA DE LA LUZ

Spain's southern Atlantic coastline is now being discovered by foreign tourists. It runs from the Straits of Gibraltar, through the province of Cádiz to the border with Portugal at Ayamonte. The Costa de la Luz is characterised by bright blue skies – the name means the Coast of Light – modest beach developments, an abundance of fish restaurants, and the vivid culture of eastern Andalucia, the land of sherry, flamenco and bullfights.

Spanish seaside resorts run the length of the coast. At the interesting town of El Puerto de Santa María, a British company is constructing a large marina with property attached, the rather unfortunately named 'Puerto Sherry'. Most foreign visitors know the area south of Cádiz, however, and the small towns of Zahara de los Atunes and Conil de la Frontera. The former has a broad unspoilt beach and quiet location with a handful of villas and apartments for sale. Conil is rapidly turning into a medium-sized, hectic resort. Other small towns are developing slowly along the coast, and the stretch north of Tarifa is particularly popular with windsurfers.

Inland, Cádiz province has a number of mountain towns, known as the *pueblos blancos*, for their white appearance characteristic of Andalucia. These offer some of the best secluded rural homes in Spain, in beautiful surroundings and close to the main cities of Cádiz and Seville. Some new building is already taking place in these rural areas in the mountains which rise behind Gibraltar, and a number of foreign residents have bought into towns like Grazalema, El Bosque, Castellar de la Frontera, Alcála de los Gazules, Vejer de la Frontera and Medina Sidonia.

North of Cádiz, in Huelva province, there is a line of modest Spanish seaside resorts set on flat, golden beaches. To reach this part of the coast, you must make the somewhat awkward drive inland to Seville, since there is no road across the flat marshlands of the Guadalquivir delta. The whole coast is virtually deserted in winter, but comes to life on summer weekends when the populations of Cádiz and Seville go to the beach. Prices are low almost everywhere and the atmosphere very Spanish. In certain areas, it does seem likely that wise buyers can expect some degree of return on their investment. Puerto Sherry, while by no means inexpensive, could become a sound prospect if it becomes as fashionable as rival marinas on the Mediterranean coast. Small towns, like Zahara, have seen a steady rise in prices, and one which may be maintained if development continues at its present restrained level.

Summers are hot but relieved by the Atlantic breezes, and the sea more refreshing than the Mediterranean. Golf and marina facilities can be found near the main centres. Winters are virtually deserted, with many restaurants and hotels closing for the season from November to Easter.

Travel is something of a problem, and demands a car. There are charter and scheduled flights to Gibraltar, and scheduled flights to Seville. As stated earlier, car hire in Gibraltar is more expensive than Spain so it may be worthwhile to cross the border and pick up a car in Algeciras. Cádiz is a three to four hour car journey from Málaga airport depending on traffic conditions. There are frequent hovercraft and ferry services to Morocco from the Straits of Gibraltar.

Road links to the Costa del Sol have been somewhat fraught in recent years because of congestion on the N340. However, improvements have been in train recently and, on a good day, the journey from Málaga to Cádiz by car should take around three hours.

INLAND SPAIN AND UNDEVELOPED AREAS

If one includes the Canary and Balearic Islands, Spain is the second largest country in Europe after France. It is impossible to offer anything but pointers to inland regions which the seeker after something unusual may find interesting. The northern 'green coast' has many interesting towns and a fine shoreline in Galicia and Cantabria. The weather is often cool and damp, however, and a serious disincentive to family holidays. The Basque country, running to the French border close to Biarritz, would, deservedly, have far more visitors were it not for the separatist campaign which results in occasional, well-publicised acts of violence by the ETA movement. There are charming villages and beaches along the Bay of Biscay near San Sebastian. The north west is best reached by car through France or by ferry from Plymouth to Santander.

If your taste runs to urban properties, there are attractive old quarters in most of the famous towns of Spain where one may pick up elegant apartments for reasonable prices. A mansion in Córdoba's lovely Jewish quarter, the Judería, complete with tiled, courtyard garden, may be found for substantially less than the cost of a small London flat, *if* that is really what you are seeking. Great, old cities like Toledo, Burgos, Granada, Seville, Cuenca, Salamanca and Santiago de Compostela will provide similar bargains for those who seek a central home of character and are willing to accept the bustle, late hours and conviviality of urban Spanish life. Some people do choose to have this kind of home in Spain. Invariably, they are those with an absorbing interest in the country, its culture and its people. The patios of Córdoba and the ancient streets of Toledo *are* picturesque and entrancing, but they are not pieces of theatre enacted for the benefit of the tourist. These are real communities, bound by their own traditions and habits, keen to make a living in a harsh world, and often living close to the heart of the Catholic Church. Unlike the resident foreign communities of the coast, here life revolves around work and the struggle to survive, not lotus-eating. Foreigners living in such communities are treated with respect and, eventually, welcomed if they integrate with the locals. But living in a foreign community of this nature is very different from being part of a semi-expatriate, international society on the coast.

If rural Spain appeals then you are faced with the same complex choices. You may live next to the paddy fields of Valencia or the near desert of inland Almeria, the wild mountains of the Picos de Europa or the lunar landscape of Lanzarote. The only way to get to know these areas is to read widely and, more importantly, travel as much as you can.

Like many Western countries, Spain is undergoing a gradual shift from the countryside into the cities. The long, arduous hours of agricultural life are being abandoned for the more profitable and less rigorous jobs of modern, urban existence.

Some farming communities in Spain are visibly withering away, particularly those in remote, sometimes spectacular, locations. Properties in these areas may be had for a song, but they will only appeal to people seeking total solitude and capable of living without many of the basic facilities of life, including running water. No two rural towns and villages are the same. Some, notably in the south, have adapted to a new agricultural climate well, growing exotic fruit and vegetables which fetch higher market prices than conventional crops. Other rural communities are poor, insular and narrow-minded.

If an out-of-the-way rural village appeals, make very sure that you spend some time there in all seasons before buying and come to know something of its character, the state of its local economy, and the attitude of the local people towards foreigners.

*Average temperatures in Spain (Fahrenheit/Centigrade)
Bold figures are for maximum recorded temperatures.*

Town & Area	Jan/Mar	Apr/Jun	Jul/Sep	Oct/Dec
Cape Bagur: Costa Brava	**58/15** 44/7	**68/20** 55/15	**78/26** 66/18	**63/17** 49/9
Barcelona: Costa Dorada	**58/14** 45/9	**71/22** 58/15	**80/27** 68/20	**62/16** 53/12
Valencia: Co. del Azahar	**62/16** 44/7	**74/23** 56/13	**83/28** 66/19	**67/19** 52/11
Alicante: Costa Blanca	**64/18** 45/7	**78/26** 56/13	**88/31** 67/19	**70/22** 51/11
Málaga: Costa del Sol	**64/18** 50/10	**76/24** 60/16	**84/29** 70/21	**68/20** 54/12
Cádiz: Costa de la Luz	**60/16** 48/9	**75/24** 60/16	**84/29** 67/20	**69/20** 54/12
Santander: Cantabria	**55/13** 46/7	**63/24** 53/15	**71/22** 62/16	**59/15** 50/10
Pontevedra: Galicia	**59/15** 40/4	**69/21** 50/10	**77/25** 55/13	**63/17** 44/6
Madrid: Castille	**54/12** 37/3	**73/23** 54/12	**81/28** 61/16	**57/14** 43/5
Seville: Inland Andalucia	**64/18** 45/7	**83/27** 57/14	**94/34** 67/20	**69/20** 52/10
Mallorca: Balearics	**60/15** 44/7	**73/22** 57/14	**83/29** 66/19	**66/18** 52/10
Las Palmas: Canaries East	**71/21** 61/16	**74/23** 65/18	**78/26** 71/22	**77/24** 66/19
Tenerife: Canaries West	**70/21** 58/14	**76/24** 63/17	**83/28** 69/21	**75/23** 63/17

*Source: Spanish National Tourist Office.

3 Finding a Home

The principles of finding a home in Spain are much the same as those which apply in the rest of Europe. The differences lie in the details of property transactions, and those are mainly concerned with the law.

Spain has a large and busy estate agency sector. Like their British counterparts, Spanish estate agents work on variable sales commissions and should *always* be regarded as salesmen and women. The friendly advice which they give you will normally be genuine and accurate, but you should never forget that the agent is there to complete the deal, not to act as an independent arbiter on your behalf. People who would never dream of taking an agent's word on guarantees about uninterrupted views in England are often strangely inclined to do so once they get a touch of the Spanish sun. Don't join them in the habit – it can be rather costly.

When first considering the price range you wish to look at, do bear in mind that you should expect to pay an extra 12 per cent to 14 per cent of the purchase price in taxes, lawyer's fees and other costs. This compares with the cost of house purchases in most European countries.

Through agencies and sales offices in Spain

There is an active property market in all resort areas throughout the year. All agencies dealing in villa and apartment sales will have at least one member of staff who speaks English. You can find estate agency offices in the resort centre or ask the tourist information office for a list of addresses. A properly established agent will belong to the professional body, the Spanish college of estate agents, and say so on his or her credentials.

Although you can begin by writing to a Spanish estate agent to find out what is available in the local area, there is no substitute for a personal visit. Spanish agents are unwilling to bombard you by post with detailed sales literature about properties in the way that their British equivalents do. Visit the various agencies in the region you have selected, explain what you are looking for, your price range, and the specific locations which interest you, and examine what they have to offer.

Large developments normally run their own sales offices, dealing solely with apartments and villas on one particular estate, though they may also sell the same units through local agencies too. If this is the case, you may find that you can negotiate a better deal directly with the developer who will have to pay sizable commission to the agent if the latter introduces the purchaser. Under no circumstances pay any deposit to an agent until you have taken legal advice.

Rural homes and those in Spanish towns with little experience of foreign residents are by far the most difficult to find. Much the easiest way to track them down is from an established base in Spain, even a rented one. Resort estate agencies will have details of rural estates within a 30-mile radius or so of their office and charge you a hefty commission for using their services.

The cheapest way to find a home outside the tourist areas is to track one down yourself through the columns of local Spanish papers or through visiting the local estate agents. If you can, take a native Spanish speaker with you for some inside knowledge of the area. The arrival of a property-hunting foreigner in town is likely to be greeted with a rubbing of hands and a swift redrawing of any prices which you have not already seen. Be prepared to negotiate and to negotiate hard.

Buying privately

Property is advertised privately in both Spanish and English periodicals in Spain and in the national British press. Property sold privately *should* be keenly priced since there is no agents' margin to pay. Some small ads are on behalf of agencies or people selling on commission, however, and, in the case of ads placed in Britain, there are clearly instances where the prices quoted assume an ignorance on the part of the purchaser of the true market values of the area concerned. It is therefore useful to get some prices on similar properties in the region for comparison. This will put you in a stronger position for any negotiations. Buying privately imposes no greater theoretical risks on the transaction than going through an agent. It is, however, even more vital to involve a lawyer in the proceedings once you become seriously interested. He or she must first ensure that the person advertising the property is legally entitled to sell it, as well as checking the many other legal aspects of the sale which require attention in all cases.

Some Spanish estate agents are becoming increasingly aware of the competition of private sales, and several now offer guarantees of clean title and an absence of serious debts (see p. 59) for the properties which they list. This is a promising sign, *if* such guarantees are genuine and legally enforceable, and that depends upon both the integrity of the agency and the fine print of the offer they are making. A lawyer can advise.

Through agencies and sales offices in England

The size of the market in Spanish homes is such that a number of British estate agents now specialise in the country. A list of those registered with the Royal Institution of Chartered Surveyors and the National Association of Estate Agents is included in the appendix. This is not exclusive; Spanish homes may often appear in the windows of small estate agencies which have decided to place them on their books. A number of specialist Spanish property shows and exhibitions now travel round the country offering inspection flights to a range of developments in tourist areas on the mainland and in the Balearics and Canaries.

Talking to a number of specialist British estate agents will give you an idea of the kind of prices you might expect to pay for different homes in various parts of Spain. Some of those on offer will have come directly to the agent; others will appear through a relationship he has forged with an agency in Spain. In the latter case, you may be asked to pay more commission than would apply if you tracked down the same property in Spain through the original agent involved. You will not make yourself popular with the estate agent concerned, but it is always a good idea to try to find out what is being asked for the same property in Spain. Occasionally, the difference can be startling, as much as 20 per cent in one case known to the author.

Large developments, such as Sotogrande and El Capistrano, usually have a contract with one of the bigger British estate agents who can arrange viewing flights to the *urbanización* with the promise of a refund of the cost of the tickets if you buy. This kind of offer is perfectly above board, but it does attempt to close your options somewhat before you leave. Nor are the cheap air tickets on offer usually any more of a bargain than you might find by scouring the small travel ads of the national press. Travelling independently and visiting a variety of developments under your own steam will remove you from the grasp of professional salesmen and women and give you a more accurate picture of the environment and character of the area in which the property is situated. Having made your choice and discovered any extra costs involved, you may then return to England and complete the transaction through a British agency if you prefer.

4 Buying Spanish Property

One day property laws and the rules governing the transfer of foreign currencies will be the same across Europe. Until then, the buyer of a foreign home, whatever the country, must accept that he or she faces a complex tangle of law and bureaucracy, most of it in a foreign language, which only the experts can unravel.

I must emphasise once more that only the foolhardy will attempt to buy property in Spain without resorting to independent professional advice, not the word of an estate agent, however reputable – nor is this book designed to be a replacement for the services of a good lawyer or accountant. Apart from the financial hazards, you should bear in mind that there are many practical difficulties which accompany the purchase of a foreign home, particularly if you intend to use it as a primary residence. Repairs, local taxation, furnishings, telephones, electricity, gas, water supplies... the list may seem endless.

The last thing you will want is to have to deal with everyday practicalities just when the purchase contract becomes bogged down in technical details which defy the comprehension of mere mortals, even those with day-to-day knowledge of the language concerned.

As one might expect, Spanish property law is quite unlike its English equivalent. The purpose of this section is not to outline, in minute detail, the many differences involved, but to give you a broad understanding of the most important principles and common terms involved in property transactions so that you can raise them with your professional adviser where necessary.

You do *not* need to understand how Spanish property law works in order to buy property or land in Spain. You *do* need to know how to go about locating sound professional advice to guide you through the transaction. A reliable and trustworthy lawyer is of far more value than a thorough knowledge of the arcane terms and practices of Spanish property law.

Given the publicity surrounding property problems in Spain, the case for employing a lawyer should be self evident. Yet a survey by the Foreign Property Owners' Institute in 1984 revealed that only 14 per cent of its members had used a lawyer for their property purchases. It is hard to escape the conclusion that many of the difficulties experienced by property buyers in Spain stem from this basic omission.

LOOKING FOR PROFESSIONAL ADVICE

It is exceedingly frustrating to be told that the best way to find professional advice in Spain, or indeed any foreign country, is by word of mouth. What everyone wants is a simple central agency which will supply guaranteed solicitors, accountants, financial advisers or even dentists, to order. No such agency exists in Spain (or anywhere else as far as I am aware).

The names of lawyers are readily available from local tourist offices and British consulates. Normally, they will be Spanish lawyers who speak good English and have a background in handling property transactions for foreign nationals. A few English lawyers specialise in Spanish property transactions and can do the job equally well. They can be reached through the Law Society, detailed in the information section of the book, or by contacting a local solicitor in England who will then sub-contract the work to an expert. There is much to be said for dealing with a lawyer who is located close to the area where you intend to buy; the jungle of Spanish red tape is best negotiated at close hand, particularly for complex transactions. If you are planning to open an account with a British bank branch the manager will also be able to recommend an English-speaking lawyer with knowledge of property transactions.

British consulates will also provide you with a list of local, English-speaking lawyers, as will most municipal tourist offices. Addresses and phone numbers for both consulates and tourist offices are given in the appendix. Useful as lists from these sources may be, they cannot replace a personal recommendation based upon actual experience.

There are plenty of people in Spain who will be only too happy to guide you for free. In most of the areas where foreigners buy property, you will find that thousands have done the same before you, and have learnt from their own mistakes. The simplest way to profit from their experiences is to ask their advice. There is nothing an expatriate resident likes better than being able to offer a few words of guidance to a prospective newcomer. All resort areas have several different social organisations, which may be a branch of the Rotary Club, or, in the case of the Costa del Sol, a local Conservative Association. Contact the secretary of the group concerned, go to their next gathering and take a notebook.

One of the first questions you should ask of your chosen lawyer is how much he will charge for handling the transaction. There are no real set scales of fees for such work in Spain, and the final bill will depend very much on the amount of work required. Simple freehold transactions are cheaper than complicated leasehold ones. In general, lawyers' fees may amount to between one and three per cent of the purchase price of the property if the contract is not unduly complicated.

WHEN TO FIND YOUR LAWYER

A lawyer becomes vital once you have found the property you are looking for and have negotiated a price for it which is agreeable to both parties. However, it is wise not to wait until your ideal property has materialised before looking for a suitable legal representative for the transaction. The law in Spain, as elsewhere, moves slowly, particularly during the summer months, and delays can be frustrating.

Try to find someone who will represent you when you begin your search, and return to him or her when you have found the property you would like to purchase. You will already have formed a relationship with the lawyer in question and will usually find that the transaction will run more smoothly than it might for someone who just walks through the door looking for instant service.

Some sellers in Spain will tell you that the employment of lawyers for both sale and purchase is a waste of money and suggest that you share the costs of one lawyer. They may be making this offer with the best of intentions, but under *no* circumstances agree to it. The interests of purchaser and vendor are axiomatically at variance, so it is essential that each side in the transaction has its own representative ensuring that a full range of checks and safeguards against debt and planning irregularities is made.

PAYING FOR YOUR HOME

One principle should be established when you buy your first home in Spain – the right to get your investment out of the country again when you sell the property. A good lawyer must make this point to you at an early stage, and an experienced estate agent will do the same, sometimes with an offer – which you should decline – to supply a lawyer who will handle the transaction for both parties.

At the time of writing, Spain is a country which has a system of exchange control to limit the movement of its own capital outside the country's national borders. Exchange control has not been seen in Britain since the late 1970s and most people have now forgotten how the system works. You *must* take note of the exchange control situation which applies when you buy or risk trapping your investment in Spain for good. Free movement of capital within Europe is one of the goals of the EEC but it does not apply at the time of writing, and may not necessarily do so even after the much-vaunted date of 1992 when harmonisation of the member states is meant to begin in earnest.

The principles are relatively simple. Money which you have imported into Spain for the purpose of buying property can, in the right circumstances, be re-exported, with a profit and after the necessary taxes have been deducted, if you eventually decide to sell. The key points to watch are your status – resident or non-resident – and the currency in which the transaction takes place. The main principle behind the rules is that residents may usually only sell for pesetas and must keep within Spain investment which was raised there.

This is not necessarily restrictive. For example, the commonest way to buy property in Spain, live as a resident *and* be able to take out the money on selling works like this. You buy the property as a non-resident, bringing in foreign exchange which is converted to pesetas for the sale. The bank supplies a certificate to prove that the money for the transactions has been imported. You move in, become resident and live in the property for as long as you like. When you want to leave, you revert to non-resident status – this is simply a matter of surrendering your identity card – and sell. As a non-resident you may now sell to a foreigner and take out of the country a sum equivalent to your original investment plus a 'reasonable profit', reasonable, that is, to the state taxation authorities. The transaction will normally be in pesetas but 'converted' ones which may be legally taken out of the country.

Buying and selling as a non-resident is the preferred way of dealing with a property transaction. However, sometimes you may find sellers who insist on being paid in a foreign currency. This is perfectly legal, although it does not absolve you from paying the relevant Spanish taxes. However, if you buy directly in foreign currency and then sell in pesetas you will not be able to take the proceeds out of the country, since the original investment was never converted. You can keep the proceeds if you find a buyer who will also pay in foreign currency. You are, effectively, in a chain of purchasers who are only interested in foreign currency sales – and so your market is more limited.

These basic guidelines are used by most buyers, even those who do not wish to return to Britain but, at the same time, are keen not to have their original investment trapped within Spanish borders. Spanish foreign exchange law is infinitely more complex than this, of course, and should be left to qualified experts to deal with in detail. It is also likely to change over the years to come. An accountant or financial adviser used to dealing with foreign exchange problems is essential. British banks in Spain commonly offer investment advice services.

Borrowing for property buying

If you cannot or do not want to pay the full amount from your own pocket, where do you borrow the balance from? Usually you will be looking to a bank, and it is now possible to arrange mortgages in Spain, in Britain, or even through another country. Several British building societies are also in the market for lending for Spanish properties, and they offer much the same rates and services as their banking rivals.

The guiding force in your decision is simply the rate of interest involved. There is no inherent advantage to be gained from taking out a mortgage in Spain; even if the Spanish home is your primary residence you will not receive any tax relief on mortgage interest. A Spanish mortgage in pesetas is subject to more restrictions than one issued in Spain or elsewhere in foreign currency. A peseta mortgage is principally for the purchase of new housing, although discretionary exceptions are allowed by the authorities, and it must not be granted at more favourable terms than those which apply to residents. Foreign currency mortgages can be used for property of any age, and may have better rates. Whoever is lending the money, whether it is a local bank or a British finance house, their primary consideration will be your ability to repay the loan or, failing that, their ability to recoup the balance outstanding through reclaiming the property over which they have a mortgage.

With branches of Banco Natwest March, the largest British-linked bank chain in Spain, the term of a loan may run up to 15 years with a 'capital holiday', during which only interest is paid, of up to two years. Repayments may be monthly, quarterly or six-monthly equal instalments, partial or total repayments can be made without penalty, and a flat fee commission of half a per cent on the mortgage is charged. The rate of interest for peseta borrowings is one per cent above the bank's one-year preferential base rate; that for sterling at two per cent over the London Interbank offered rate (LIBOR) fixed twice yearly. The latter *may* be cheaper.

The bank will lend up to 70 per cent of the mortgage valuation of the property provided the applicant's total mortgage borrowing does not exceed two and a half times his proven gross annual income, and that the total annual term commitments are not more than 25 per cent of his income. These are fairly standard terms which you could expect to see reflected by other banks in Spain interested in non-resident custom.

Many British banks are quite happy to loan sums to their customers to pay for second homes and you may think this the simplest solution. They will also lend money to people whose primary residence is in Spain and second home is in Britain. Some kind of security will be demanded for all loans; in Spain, it will normally be a charge over the property itself. In Britain, this may be impractical and you could be expected to guarantee the loan through your primary or secondary residence.

Banks in Spain and Britain will tell you their current interest rates for this kind of loan and normally work out the monthly repayments for you. Interest rates are volatile and can give you nasty shocks. Do your best to understand interest rate trends at the time you buy, talking to a financial adviser if necessary. Do not assume that the rate which you begin with will be the one which you will be paying six months or a year later.

Nor should you fall for some of the 'offers' seen in time of high interest rates which guarantee the rate of the loan will not rise for, say, two years or so. These often come out of the woodwork at a time when interest rates are beginning to peak and the unwary do not realise that a fall is just around the corner. Fixed interest rate deals are usually poor bargains for the customer at times of higher interest; you may well find yourself sitting on the higher rate when everyone else has watched theirs go down.

Developers of new *urbanizaciónes* will often offer finance directly to the customer. Usually this is through an arrangement which they have negotiated with a friendly bank – you are not borrowing directly from the contractor. Developer funds are rarely more advantageous than those which you can arrange yourself directly through a bank. Compare the interest rate on offer with what you might get elsewhere. You should also ensure that there are no punitive clauses which prevent you, for example, repaying the entire sum early at a discount or penalise you unfairly if you miss a payment.

THE LEGAL FRAMEWORK

The finer points of property law can and should be left to your lawyer, but there is one important principle which should be borne in mind in any Spanish property transaction. In the United Kingdom, and many other countries, the purchase of private property is a transaction which produces a 'clean' exchange of title between the vendor and purchaser. In other words, the buyer, in closing the deal, normally takes on the property alone, not the responsibility for any charges associated with it before he became the owner.

In Spain, property purchase follows a principle similar to that used for company purchases in the United Kingdom. When you buy a property, you receive not only the bricks and mortar and all the other assets associated with it but *also* all the outstanding debts. This principle is the single greatest cause of heartache in the worst cases of property problems in Spain.

In minor cases, the bill is small and annoying – a local tax or electricity bill outstanding from the previous owner which he should have paid. Sometimes, it is not even the former occupant's fault – a Spanish service company has failed to issue an invoice in time and you, as the new owner, will be billed for what your predecessor used. In these cases you may fume and argue... but in the end you will have to pay, and possibly pay even more, in the form of penalties, if you delay settling the bill too long.

Sometimes the consequences are more serious.

> 'A Briton bought a villa on the Cala Blanca estate near Alicante in 1982. He paid the developer the full purchase price and received an *escritura* from the notary and the Land Registry at Denia stating the property to be free of all charges. Two years later he – and 40 other owners in the same situation – discovered that their property was mortgaged in favour of the Banco Hipotecario from which the developer had borrowed to finance the construction of the villas. The amount of the mortgage – 1.5 million pesetas on each villa – should have been paid off by the developer on payment of the purchase price. However, the developer did not do so, nor did the bank make any effort to recover the money from the developer. The owner himself paid off the mortgage, plus interest, in order to avoid having his villa sold by the bank at public auction.
>
> 'The same story is repeated at the nearby Els Pins Park at

Moraira, and it is only the forbearance of the Banco Hipotecario – which is awaiting the outcome of criminal *denuncias* against the developers – which allows the 54 residents to stay in their homes, although interest charges are building up and the properties cannot be resold without paying off the mortgages, which total 65 million pesetas.'

McMillan-Scott report, January 1989

Stories like these – where enormous hidden debts appear after a property has apparently been cleared by the authorities – are extremely rare, and it should be remembered that property transactions in Britain can also lead to similar disasters. But cases in which debts, sometimes amounting to thousands of pounds, have been missed by purchasers, either acting on their own or through an inefficient lawyer, are far from uncommon.

There is rarely any legal remedy in these instances. Even if criminal proceedings ensue, you will doubtless find that the money you paid for the property has already been transferred by the vendor to an account which cannot be reached by the authorities, perhaps to a relative or abroad.

Employing a lawyer, preferably one found through personal recommendation, should guarantee that thorough checks are made to discover hidden debts, and you are given a full report about any which are found. No lawyer can track down every last bill connected with a property, and you may well find the telephone or electricity company will chase you for a debt of the previous occupant. Major sums for building work and maintenance are a different matter and should be uncovered by any competent lawyer as part of the investigation process discussed later. Should such debts materialise *after* your lawyer's investigations, then you are in a position to claim against the lawyer for negligence or ask for arbitration from his professional organisation, in the case of Spain, the *Ilustre Colegio de Abogados*, the equivalent of the English Law Society. Such claims are no easier to win in Spain than in Britain, and should be regarded as a last resort. Membership of professional organisations is more a guarantee of expert qualifications than a system for pursuing compensation claims when transactions go wrong and you feel the lawyer is at fault.

Non-completion of estates

The second common problem of the foreign buyer is the failure on the part of a developer to complete an *urbanización*. This can be extremely distressing and depress the value of the property for many years.

> 'In 1981 Mr Claudio Evrard (German) claims that he paid the promoter a first instalment of 40 per cent towards the purchase price of a house on the Cap Blanc development near Peñiscola. In 1983 the development company got into financial difficulty and asked the buyers to pay the outstanding instalments of 20 per cent and 40 per cent in return for the signature of the *escritura*, although the houses had not yet been completed. The buyers paid the balance because they feared that the company would otherwise simply go into liquidation and their investment would be lost. In the event, although Mr Evrard got his house, the promoter did not build the roads and pavements contracted for, which he and the other owners had to pay for themselves. The development as a whole is illegal (lacks planning consent) and so cannot be connected to the electricity supply although its illegality does not prevent the town hall from levying local taxes.'
>
> *McMillan-Scott report, January 1989*

'Illegal' buildings – ones which have been erected without planning permission and then sold on the open market as if they had been properly erected – are behind many of the cautionary tales about Spanish property. If you use a lawyer for the transaction, you should have an absolute guarantee that the property has been erected with the consent of the local authorities. However in this case, illegality is only part of the problem. The position in which the unfortunate Mr Evrard found himself is one which, potentially, could affect many buyers today.

New developments are usually marketed before the full *urbanización* is finished. This stems from a customary and understandable wish on the part of the developer to claw back a little cash flow into his company as early as possible. The customer can benefit from this. Many people have taken out options to buy units in developments before the builder has even finished the first home. In return, they have been given substantial discounts, sometimes as much as 25 per cent, off the opening price of homes... and sometimes gone on to make large profits in only a few years.

The outcome is distinctly less happy if the developer runs into problems. He may be unable to finish the infrastructure of the estate or even the very houses themselves, leaving the customer with little more than a stake in a building plot. In other cases, the builder may even have a bank charge over the estate which gives the bank ownership of the estate even including properties which have been paid for – to the developer – by residents (see pp. 59-60).

Clearly, buying a unit in an estate which has not yet been finished involves risks. The principal one is of insolvency on the part of the developer. Judge for yourself the experience and reputation of the firm concerned by asking about how long it has been in business and how many other estates it has erected. A number of long-established British-based builders are now active in Spain and are unlikely to disappoint their customers. New, small construction companies are more vulnerable since they may not have such large reserves to fall back upon if the market takes a downturn.

It is not unusual for developments to change hands several times from conception to completion, and this even happens to large ones such as Puerto Sherry near Cádiz which has seen several owners in its brief existence. A change of ownership is usually good news – at least someone wants to proceed with the scheme. You do not need to look far along the Spanish coast to discover that there are many smaller projects which have faltered halfway through leaving unfinished breezeblock skeletons along the shoreline. Take time to inquire into the background of your *urbanización*'s builder; it could help ensure that your money is not paying for one more such skeleton.

Some developers offer bank guarantees against failure to deliver which promise your investment back if the development is not completed. Read these carefully. They will usually be a form of insurance policy with the bank which *you*, not the developer, pay for.

THE *LEY DE COSTAS*

In early 1989, some British newspapers ran stories about a new law, the *ley de costas*, interpreting it as a threat to 'nationalise' half a million British-owned homes in Spain. The law was also represented by at least one national newspaper as an indication that Spain wished to discourage foreign home-owning and make itself less reliant on tourism for its foreign exchange earnings.

The truth is somewhat more mundane and it illustrates, once more, the necessity of getting good legal advice to avoid the perils of illegal properties. The *ley de costas* is certainly something which you should consider *if* you intend to buy a property in one of the coastal areas affected. For those in illegal developments, the consequences may be serious. However, the chief purpose of the law is to protect the Spanish coastline and end the kind of unrestricted development which has ruined many miles of seashore. Many will regard it as a timely and welcome measure, once the legal position of residents in affected areas has been made clear.

The first thing which should be understood about the law is that it affects *all* residents, foreign and Spanish, equally. Since June 1988, when it came into effect, new building has been banned along a 100-metre deep strip around the whole of Spain's coastline. Developments which have been erected legally within this strip are unaffected by the law. An illegal home, however, can be expropriated by the state and demolished unless for reasons of public interest it should be legalised. A concession was made for private owners of illegal homes affected. They are allowed the use of the property for up to 30 years, with the possibility of a further 30 years extension. If the state does demolish private homes, the owners will be compensated.

The majority of those affected by the law are Spaniards who built weekend cottages on plots of land they owned by the beach. Anyone who has purchased an illegally built home in the affected area will be penalised as if he or she were the original culprit, however, and some foreigners fall into this category.

It is very easy to discover if a property might be affected by the law. If it is legal, then it is safe. If it is illegal and within 100 metres of the shoreline, then under no circumstances consider buying it. If it is illegal but outside the affected area then the *ley de costas* will not affect you but other problems most likely will. Some illegal development is later legalised, but no-one, least of all a developer, can guarantee that this will happen. You buy illegal property at your peril.

THE SALES CONTRACT

Once you have found your perfect property and agreed the price, your lawyer should begin the task of investigating its past, present and future and commissioning a building survey to ensure that there are no structural defects to worry you. Rising damp and deathwatch beetle are the least of a Spanish property purchaser's worries. Building defects are normally visible to the eye of the most untrained visitor, and the lawyer's investigations should turn up any hidden ones. It is not normally necessary to order a separate property survey on common resort properties. More common problems tend to do with the payment of bills by the previous owner and the intentions of the local planning department. Did the last owner pay his municipal taxes? Does the charming vendor really have full title to sell the property? Is a new hypermarket about to be built in the pine wood at the bottom of the garden?

All of these thing should become clear as your *abogado*, or a junior colleague, sifts through the official papers. Beyond seeking assurances that there are no hidden debts or unforeseen building plans in the area, you should leave the job to the professionals. Once your lawyer is happy with the conditions of the sale, you will be presented with an official purchase contract, the *escritura de compraventa* and usually asked to make a deposit on the property. The terms of the contract will determine whether the deposit is returnable or not. In a simple transaction, you might get the keys to your new home – and the full bill – in a matter of weeks; more complex ones can take months.

The *escritura de compraventa* must be signed in the presence of a *notario*, a public official who enters the transaction into the property register. The *notario* is an unbiased agent in these matters and does not offer advice to either party. You will often be offered two contracts, one in English, the second in Spanish.

Only the Spanish document is a legally binding contract, and it will be retained by the *notario* for safe keeping.

In the contract the price will be stated in pesetas. If you have changed foreign currency into pesetas to pay for the sale you should have a certificate from your bank recording the foreign exchange transaction, which will be noted in the official records. This piece of paper can be very important. Without it you will not be able to prove that the original fee was imported into Spain for the purpose of buying property; and if you cannot prove that you will not be able to take the proceeds of your eventual sale of the property out of Spain again (see p. 55).

You will normally gain possession of the property once the *escritura de compraventa* has been signed in front of the *notario* and the balance of the purchase price paid to the vendor. However, the transaction is not officially complete until later when the contract has been entered into the public property register, the *registro de la propiedad*. At this stage the *escritura de compraventa* will be converted into a formal title deed which names you as the official owner of the property. Until you receive the final document, you will be given a first copy of the *escritura* – the *copia simple*. This will serve as official evidence of your purchase until the final documentation arrives.

When the contract is signed, your lawyer will ask for a sum to be deposited to cover the property taxes and his fee which are paid when the deed is formally registered. Any unused money is returned to you when the final bills are paid. The conversion process can take some time, even several months, although it is no more than a formality in the vast majority of cases.

If it is inconvenient for you to return to Spain to sign the contract documents, you can arrange for your lawyer to sign on your behalf. The best way to do this is to ask him to organise the necessary documentation during one of your visits and sign the form, the *escritura de poder de compraventa*, while you are in Spain. Once your lawyer has this form, he is empowered to complete the contract for you. Do not hand over that power unless you are absolutely certain that you want the property. You will be taking an irrevocable step.

SALES TAXES AND FEES

The fees for using the *notario* and registering the deed of the property vary according to the size of the transaction but rarely reach two per cent of the purchase cost. In addition, you will normally have to pay a purchase tax of six per cent. This will be IVA (Valued Added Tax) if you are buying the property from a company, or *Impuesto de Transmisiones Patrimoniales* if you are buying from a private seller.

At the moment it does not matter which tax affects you, both carry the same rate, but this may change. In addition, most sellers today expect the purchaser to pay the capital gains tax – *plus valía* – involved in the deal. There is no law that says you must pay the *plus valía*, however, and this is simply a matter for negotiation in the contract.

The reckoning of the *plus valía* is complicated and depends upon how much, in the local authority's eyes, the property has appreciated in value since it was last sold. The idea of any such elastic tax in a property contract may appear somewhat daunting, but, if the thought worries you, your lawyer should be able to give you an idea of the *plus valía* which would be payable. A public register of property values is maintained at all town halls, and it is these figures which are used to assess the tax.

For reasons which are no longer applicable, property owners in Spain attempted at one time to value their homes at well below the market rate. This saved some money at the time but could lead to horrendous *plus valía* bills on selling, bills which more than a few attempted to pass on to purchasers. All properties should now be valued more realistically for reckoning the *plus valía*, and anyone who tells you otherwise about transactions in recent years is spinning a yarn.

One final tax is only applicable if you have not paid the relevant transfer tax at the time of signing the *escritura* – a stamp duty, *Impuesto sobre Actos Jurídicos Documentados*, which currently costs half a per cent of the value of the property.

It is, as stated earlier, impossible to forecast to the last peseta how much any property transaction will cost in Spain. However, as a general rule, taxes and fees normally add up to around 10 or 12 per cent of purchase price, with a further 2 per cent in lawyer's fees (if the sale was straightforward).

MAINTENANCE CHARGES

If your new property is in an estate development or an apartment block, there will normally be further charges to pay before you can move in. All communal properties will attract maintenance charges to pay for the upkeep of the estate. Spanish law determines which parts of a property are the responsibility of the individual owner and which the duty of the community. The breakdown is much the same as one would expect of a similar situation in the UK. You are, for instance, responsible for internal wiring and plumbing of your property, but the estate will maintain private street lighting and recover the cost from the community. Spanish law demands the creation of a communal organisation of residents of both apartment blocks and leasehold estates of villas. The organisation holds an annual meeting for community members and is legally empowered to recover the fees of running the estate from each individual member according to a formula based on the size of the property.

Always pay community fees, even if you want to argue about them later. The community is empowered by law to recover unpaid dues and may bar you from using your property until it has received the money. Details of the current level of fees due for a particular property should be made available when you are offered the *escritura de compraventa* for an apartment or *urbanización* property.

FOREIGN PROPERTY OWNERS' INSTITUTE

The Instituto de Proprietarios Extranjeros is, as its name implies, a body formed to advise and act for the interests of foreign residents in Spain. Sadly, the Institute itself has proved as controversial as the very issue of property exploitation which led to its formation. According to Edward McMillan-Scott, the body is the only organisation in Spain trying to help foreign property owners. Its critics, who include Spanish estate agents and former customers of the ex-property developer behind the group, regard it as a money-making venture pure and simple.

The Institute was formed in 1983 by Mr Per Svensson, a Norwegian former salesman with a great deal of experience in the Spanish housing market. It is precisely this experience, and in particular an involvement in an abortive development in the Alpujarras which lost a number of unhappy investors their funds, which has caused the controversy about the Institute. The facts of Mr Svensson's colourful career are of little interest here, and were thoroughly documented in *Lookout* magazine in June 1988 for anyone who wishes to know them.

Of more interest is the question: what can the Institute do for the foreign property owner to make the annual subscription, currently around £45, falling to £36 in subsequent years, really worthwhile? The services of the institute are:

— a free copy of Mr Svensson's book *Your Home in Spain*
— free answers to 'short, local questions'
— free advice (to questions in writing or posed in person at the organisation's head office in Calpe on the Costa Blanca)
— a 'green light service' which is a fixed document check for those about to buy property
— a free document check to ensure that day-to-day paperwork about your property is in order
— a free subscription to the organisation's monthly magazine, *Spain Today*, which normally costs 200 pesetas
— discounts on some goods and services such as insurance, property surveys, car repairs and purchase and furniture sales

How valuable is all this? Frankly, it rather depends upon the purchaser. It is no reflection on the service offered by the Institute to say that anyone who relied upon it as a primary source of advice during a property purchase would be living very dangerously indeed.

A lawyer is a skilled, trained professional, answerable to a regulatory body and finally, in the case of negligence, to the civil courts for the advice he gives and the quality of his work. The same cannot be said for an informal document-checking service, however thorough. However, a skilled eye can be very useful in spotting small, contractual problems which could arise after a purchase has occurred which may be unnecessarily expensive to resolve through professional means, and for such advice the Institute may be invaluable. Whether it is likely to offer anything which could not be gleaned on the normal bush telegraph of counsel and information which runs through any expatriate community is another matter.

The Institute is also a ready source of names and addresses for those seeking professional advice without having to track down the information personally. *Spain Today* contains a list of Institute 'delegates', in fact professionals from the fields of law, surveying and financial advice who will offer their services 'at minimum rates' to Institute members. The locale, speciality and languages of each individual is listed, along with the names and addresses of lay 'co-ordinators' and 'service offices' who will act as local contacts for members.

The idea is admirable. But it should be said that the Institute's penetration of the vast foreign residents' community is miniscule, amounting to around 18,000 members out of a community some estimate as approaching one million. The organisation is at its strongest on the Costa Blanca, where it is based, and the coverage of its magazine reflects this. Nor can *Spain Today* hold a candle, in its advice columns, to those of *Lookout*. In fact the Institute's publication is a strange beast indeed, full of small, inconsequential news items and features.

Perhaps its most useful service – and it may seem a strange one – is that it prints the names of members who have been mentioned in official provincial debtors' bulletins. This is not meant to be a list of shame, but a warning to members who may have accidentally incurred debts, usually municipal, of which they know nothing. Even a small, unacknowledged debt can bring down the weight of the law upon the unwary, innocent of the obligation though they may be.

Membership of the Institute is not prohibitively expensive – and the standing order can be cancelled after the first year. If you are uncertain of finding local advice on your own, the Institute could be an easy preliminary way into foreign resident circles.

5   Renting Property

THE TENANT'S VIEW

It is extremely easy to rent properties in all the tourist areas of Spain. This is often an admirable way to get to know a town or region that interests you without having to make the commitment to purchase. It is also a sound alternative to timeshare, as will be shown later. Before you buy, you may want to pause for thought about why the rental market is so large in Spain. The answer: because a great many foreign-owned properties are left empty for much of the time.

Rental prices are, in general, very reasonable, far more so than one would think from the costs quoted in the small ad sections of British newspapers. To pick up the bargains, and make sure that you know what you are taking on, you will need to make the arrangement locally. Except during the height of the season, one can normally guarantee to find an apartment in any of the main resort towns just by calling around estate agents, examining the columns of local papers, and asking in any English-owned shops, restaurants or bars. As you would expect, the price per week falls, sometimes dramatically, the longer you are willing to rent the property. Sumptuous villas can, on occasion, be picked up for little more than the cost of a hotel room because the owners are unable to visit them in that season.

Strictly speaking, you should sign a contract for any apartment lease. This is a legal document which will stipulate the length of your tenancy, the price you are going to pay and any deposits demanded by the owner. Most rentals by foreigners are *por temporada*, in other words, temporary. This is more a description of the rights which you have as a tenant than a time restriction on the letting. Long-term occupants are covered by different regulations to temporary tenants, even though the latter may often occupy the property for a year or more.

However, for short lets many owners will ask little more than a deposit and keep the transaction – and the profits – unofficial. In this case, keep receipts for your rental payments so that you have some proof that you are entitled to use the property.

THE LANDLORD'S VIEW

People buying property often convince themselves that part of the price will be paid for from rental income. You *can* offset the costs of your Spanish home in this way, but you need to proceed carefully to safeguard your interests as a landlord. Nor is income from rentals free from tax. You will normally be liable for Spanish tax on rental income if you reach the taxable limits on *all* your income derived in Spain, at the time of writing 840,000 pesetas a year. If, like most buyers, you buy a property on a convertible account bringing in funds from abroad, you will *not* be allowed to use the income from renting to pay the mortgage. The reasoning is simple: you are bringing in foreign exchange funds to pay for the purchase, in return for eventual concessions in being able to take your investment out of Spain again. The money raised by lettings, however, is income earned within Spain – and cannot be included in the same category.

In terms of security, there is no doubt about the safest way to let your property for extra income: rent it out to friends, colleagues, or other people through contacts made at work or through social circles. Spread the word through advertisements on noticeboards and in staff publications, and produce a potted portrait of the property, with pictures, to show to anyone who is interested. If you can find five or six customers for a fortnight each year, at an average of, say, £250 a week, for a two-bedroom villa you will more than pay the running costs and make a little on the top.

Letting property to short-term holidaymakers, preferably those with whom you have some contact, however tenuous, is the best guarantee that your tenants leave when they should and do not cause much in the way of damage to furniture or other household belongings.

Some people are better at selling their holiday homes than others. If you have neither the time nor the inclination to do the job yourself, you may be able to reach an agreement with a holiday company to market the property on your behalf. Self-catering holiday companies advertise in the travel pages of many national newspapers, selling specific weeks in selected properties in return for a commission. They are usually only interested in villas or apartments which are of good quality and outside the large resorts where holidaymakers are well catered for by the mass package holiday companies. The convenience of allowing a third party to sell, manage and bill customers for using your property can be very attractive for those without the time or inclination to do the job themselves. All you will need to do is make available your property for agreed dates and keep it in good condition; in return, the company will pay you an agreed sum for each week in which it can let the home.

Estate agents and specialist accommodation agencies in Spain will also undertake to let your property in return for an agreed commission. Some of the larger *urbanizaciónes* have a letting service which deals directly with the public. Think carefully before you agree to such an arrangement unless you are able to monitor in person how well the property is being managed. Many owners have been bitterly disappointed by the way their holiday homes were treated by anonymous tenants with little regard for furnishings or cleanliness. You may discover that the income involved in no way compensates for the annoyance and inconvenience of letting.

Ensure that the period of any letting is set out in writing in the contract confirming the tenancy. There should be a fixed charge in the letting price to cover the use of electricity. Experienced landlords will always remove a telephone before allowing in a tenant, or expect to face a hefty phone bill a few months later, when the former tenant is usually many miles distant.

6 Timeshare Properties

Timesharing is a relatively new concept in holiday property ownership. It originated in the French Alps in the 1960s when the Societé de Grands Travaux de Marseille offered shares in a property with the slogan, 'Don't book a holiday, buy the hotel, it's cheaper'.

This distinctly questionable premise has since launched a worldwide industry which has never been far from controversy. Timeshare has been blighted by many problems, ranging from unsatisfactory building standards through to simple fraud. Any visitor to a modern Spanish resort is likely to come face to face with timeshare whether he or she likes it or not, thanks to the unwanted administrations of armies of young, principally British, salesmen and women who pester anyone they can find to visit the many new timeshare developments now being built, offering dubious 'free' gifts as an inducement.

The Costa del Sol and the Canary Islands are particularly plagued by this kind of unscrupulous, and occasionally threatening, form of marketing. Complaints about it are regularly lodged with local tourist offices who have, in many cases, asked for action from the authorities. The worst offenders are, almost invariably, North European companies using pressure selling techniques which would be illegal in their home countries, and a number of well-known British building names are by no means guiltless.

Yet for all its poor image, it remains indisputable that there are a good many happy timeshare customers who would not otherwise have been able to afford the facilities which they have bought through their contract. The Spanish Department of

Tourism commissioned a survey of timeshare owners in 1988 and came to the conclusion that 84 per cent were 'very satisfied' with their purchase while only six per cent were displeased.

The same survey leaves no doubt about the size of the timeshare business in Spain. It estimates that by the end of 1987 there were 132 timeshare complexes in Spain, 49 of them in Andalucia. More than half were one or two bedroomed apartments, 30 per cent studios, and 17 per cent villas, proof, if it were needed, that the vast majority of timeshare complexes concentrate on inexpensive, basic accommodation, similar to the kind of apartments which may be booked through self-catering package holiday companies. The British are the chief purchasers of timeshare properties, accounting for 90 per cent of the market, and British companies the main promoters of timeshare developments.

Timeshare is booming. The Timeshare Developers Association reported a 30 per cent increase in sales among its members during 1988. By 1989, the organisation forecast, some 156,000 UK residents would have a stake in timeshare, many of them in Spain.

No property purchase in Spain can be undertaken lightly, but timeshare, more than any other, requires great care. One simple rule must always apply... *never, never decide on impulse to visit a timeshare development at the invitation of a street salesman.* Most of the timeshare complexes being hawked by these people are based around a slick selling technique designed to pressure you into committing yourself to an on-the-spot contract to buy. The techniques applied to the unwary all too often are successful. You may be told that a special low price cannot be held for longer than a day, or that the option in question has just been returned by someone who needs the money quickly. These are always a form of subterfuge intended, quite simply, to extract cash for a deposit and a legally binding contract from you without further ado.

It may sound extraordinary that any holidaymaker would, on impulse, accept an invitation to visit a timeshare complex and, with little more thought, contract an option for an apartment which is irreversible and demands an instant cash payment. However, this is by no means uncommon, and there are even cases where holidaymakers have been talked into parting with all their available holiday cash in return for a 'chance of a lifetime' timeshare option, and then have to ask their tour company or the British consulate to repatriate them.

Street canvassing, though approved by the industry's self-regulatory body if it is 'courteous' and 'without undue pressure', is the cause of many complaints to tour operators and local tourist bodies. It seems likely, and highly desirable, that the Spanish authorities will take steps in the near future to control, or completely ban, timeshare canvassers from operating in this way. In the meantime, the easiest way to avoid this problem is to turn down the invitations on the spot, and complain to the local tourist office, giving them the name of the offending company, if you feel that you have been harassed.

If timeshare genuinely interests you, then take the trouble to understand how it works, seek out the timeshare properties in the areas which interest you, and compare facilities and prices. For all the reports in booming sales, remember that timeshare remains a buyers' market, if only because the commodity in question must be sold no fewer than 50 times – once for each week of the year with a respite of a week or two for maintenance.

HOW TIMESHARE WORKS

It is very simple to see what attracts property developers to timeshare. In a normal development, the builder's income comes from one source: the asking price of each unit. Once the unit is sold, then the principal source of income disappears. Timeshare, however, enables the developer to sell the property several times over, by merchandising the right to use the unit to different purchasers for one or two weeks during the year. The price per unit depends upon the season – high summer weeks often costing four or five times more than winter weeks in the case of beach resorts. Then there is a separate annual service and maintenance charge.

Once the initial contract fee has been paid, the purchaser has the right to use the unit for those particular weeks for a long or even indefinite period – *but, in most timeshare contracts, at no stage does he or she in any sense own the property.* The furnishing, decoration and equipping of the apartment is the sole responsibility of the complex owner. You will not be allowed to decorate it to your own taste or carry out alterations, even if they are agreed by other users of the same unit during other weeks of the year. Timeshare is more a form of long-term property rental than ownership. Examine any timeshare brochure and you can see why developers love it. The total gained from the sale of all timeshare weeks of one unit will often exceed the property market value of the same apartment by several hundred per cent... *and* the developer retains title to the property and continues to gain income from service charges to 'owners' in return for running the complex.

So what are the advantages of timeshare? The selling point of most organisations is the offer of an inflation-free, guaranteed holiday home, usually for the rest of your life, and one which may be used flexibly, according to your needs. You can sell your timeshare holiday to a third party or exchange your timeshare week for a timeshare holiday elsewhere.

Perhaps you are unable to take up your timeshare weeks. You may then pass them on to friends or relatives, or rent them out. And, because you have viewed the timeshare development before buying, you know precisely what you will be getting for your money in the decades to come.

These advantages are clearly very convincing for a great many people; there are currently some five million holders of timeshare certificates worldwide, the majority in north America. However, there are several disadvantages to timeshare and one alternative widely ignored by potential purchasers to their ultimate cost.

Timeshare versus rental

If you are looking at timeshare and decided upon a particular resort area to visit, do make sure that you also examine the alternative of renting an apartment. Rented accommodation is widely available in all Spanish resorts at very reasonable prices during all but the peak weeks of the season. It can offer a viable alternative to timeshare for a fraction of the outlay and none of the long-term commitment.

For example, at the time of writing, a 'shoulder' season week of timeshare – one in the summer months outside English school holidays – in a two-bedroom apartment in the Costa del Sol might cost between £4,000 and £6,000. Were you to take up the contract for a fortnight, the cost of the apartment, with maintenance at £100 per week over 15 years, would be between £11,000 and £15,000. However, the cost of renting a similar apartment through a local agent would, at current prices, rarely be more than £600 to £800 for two weeks, including all charges, and less if you are able to rent directly from the owner. There has been little inflation in rental prices in recent years, although timeshare maintenance charges can normally be guaranteed to increase yearly. Using these figures, the cost of renting a similar apartment for 15 years, even with an inflation rate over the period of 20 per cent, is roughly similar. The difference, of course, is in the timing of the money which you need to pay – with timeshare, the cash goes out at the beginning, with rental you pay as you use the accommodation.

To use rental as an alternative to timeshare, you would need to know your preferred resort well and to have good contacts with estate agents or, preferably, the property owners themselves in order to make sure that you were renting the right kind of property.

However, if, as timeshare assumes, you are going to spend most of your holidays in one location, this should not be difficult. On the other hand, you would not be able to guarantee that you have the same property each year, or benefit from exchanging your timeshare weeks with other timeshare users elsewhere. You may also find it difficult to rent the property of your choice in the peak of the season when it will normally be occupied by the owner.

On the basis of the sums used above, if you were to place £15,000 on a high rate deposit account at 9.5 per cent, you would receive net annual interest of £1,476.57, enough to pay for rental of an apartment for two weeks *and* flights for the average Spanish resort. Some of this income would be set against tax for most people, of course, but, at the end of 15 years, your £15,000 would still be there. The lesson is clear: if you have the money to pay for timeshare, there are other ways of achieving similar ends for a lower initial outlay and they should be investigated.

Resales and rental values

The Timeshare Developers Association emphasises that 'timeshare is primarily an investment in future holidays not in property, owners should not view their timeshare as a financial investment'. This thoroughly accurate assessment of the resale value of timeshare units is not always reflected in the sales talk of timeshare developers, however. Several have suggested that you can take out a timeshare contract and sell it within a reasonably short period of time at a real profit, in much the same way as property profits have been made in the United Kingdom during the property price boom of 1985-1988.

This is nonsense, and dangerous nonsense too. Timeshare units *can* be sold to other parties, and some organisations are now organising auctions precisely for this purpose at which the seller pays a commission on the sale of the timeshare unit. The complex developer will also often undertake to sell the contract, usually for a commission of 15 per cent. However, unless your contract has been held for at least 10 years, and then in a highly successful and desirable timeshare complex, it is most unlikely that you will make any genuine profit from the sale, and many people have sold for less than they originally paid simply to dispose of something which they came to realise was of no practical use to them.

In fact, your unit may well be worth less in ten years' time than it is today, even if it is held in perpetuity. Attractive as your development may be today – and most timeshare properties are of high quality – in the future it will have to compete against new timeshare developments in the market. You may judge its chances yourself. If inflation pushes up new timeshare prices considerably then there may be a market for 'second hand' contracts sold at a lower price. It seems more likely, however, that the difference in price between a unit in a new development and one in a block which is ten years' old will be minimal, and that may make your share difficult to sell at a good price.

Just as it is unwise to regard true property purchase in Spain as a guaranteed investment in the way that UK property can currently be viewed; with timeshare it is safe to say that, once your initial contract fee has been paid, your chances of recovering all of it through resale are practically nil.

The income which you may receive from renting out your property is also frequently exaggerated. If you are able to rent out the unit directly to a friend or colleague, then you should be able to charge the market rate for similar properties and avoid the commission charged by the developer if he finds someone to rent the property. But even then, after maintenance charges are taken into account, the real income is infinitesimal when compared with the scale of your original investment.

Maintenance charges

All timeshare contracts involve maintenance charges. These should be set out very clearly in the document you are asked to sign, with a ceiling limiting, in percentage terms, how much they can rise each year. And make no mistake – the maintenance charges *will* rise annually, whatever is happening to inflation. Ask the salesman to detail what the maintenance fee pays for – there should be a schedule which details the replacement of items such as furniture and electrical equipment – and try to find out what percentage increases have been levied on owners in previous years. This will give you an indication of the price trend of the development and what you will be expected to pay in the years to come.

Maintenance charges must be imposed by timeshare developers – someone has to pay for the electricity, local taxes and running costs of the estate. But they are the principal source of income for the developer once the property has been sold and as such may often come as a nasty shock to the hasty purchaser who ignored them when adding up the real cost of timeshare. You must also expect to pay maintenance charges whether you use your unit or not. The penalty for failing to pay the charges will normally be the loss of your right to use the unit under any circumstances.

Many developers now hand over the management of timeshare estates to specialised management companies who are extremely efficient at issuing invoices for maintenance fees, renting out unwanted weeks, for a commission, and running the development. There is usually no need to worry if you discover that the management has been put out to a third party company.

Exchanging your timeshare property

One of the carrots offered to potential timeshare purchasers is the ability to exchange your unit for another one of similar value when you feel like a holiday somewhere else. So, for instance, your two weeks in Marbella might be swopped for a fortnight in a timeshare resort in Miami. To do this, the development in which you have bought a unit must belong to a timeshare exchange organisation. The two largest are RCI and Interval International (II), both of which have offices in Britain (see p. 149).

Free membership of one of these organisations, for an introductory year, is often included in the price of your timeshare unit. Once this expires, you must pay an annual membership fee to be eligible for the organisation's services *and* further fees if you successfully exchange your unit for another on the group's books. Transferring to another timeshare development elsewhere in the world does *not* absolve you from the responsibility of paying the maintenance charges on your own unit. Timeshare exchanges are not free; nor is there any guarantee that you will be able to exchange your unit for the property which takes your eye in the exchange organisation's glossy brochure.

RCI currently charges a membership fee of £38 per calendar year, with discounts if you are willing to pay three or five years' membership in advance. In addition you must pay a fee for the holiday exchange itself. This is £45 per week for normal exchanges, £25 for those within the same timeshare resort, and £50 for last minute bookings. Anyone wanting to use the exchange system must deposit his or her unit weeks in the organisation's 'Spacebank'. For each week deposited – and you can store up credits for more than one year – you will become eligible to exchange the unit for a similar holding at one of RCI's affiliated resorts elsewhere in the world. If you change your mind and decide you would like your original unit back, you can only reclaim it if no other RCI member has placed a booking for it. However, if the organisation is unable to place your unit you will normally be told that it is vacant some three weeks or so beforehand. You can then occupy your unit for the time you have contracted *and* go ahead with any resort exchange which may have been arranged – two holidays for the accommodation price of one, if you like, but remember that you will only know the fate of your own timeshare unit a few weeks before you have to decide whether to occupy it.

You will normally be asked to outline a selection of preferred exchanges from the organisation's brochure. More than 30 per cent of exchanges which take place are requested a year in advance; clearly, early booking is advisable and probably essential for very popular resorts. The task of matching preferences to actual vacancies is performed by a sophisticated computer network which links RCI with its American headquarters where most timeshare transactions take place.

However, there are some important restrictions on the kinds of properties with which you may exchange and there is no guarantee that the organisation will be able to find an acceptable exchange for you at all. RCI, like most such organisations, divide the timeshare year into units according to desirability and price.

In beach resorts, the most expensive units are normally in the sunniest season; in ski resorts, at the time when there is most likely to be snow. *You can only exchange your unit for one of a similar ranking.* In other words, if you have a two week unit in January on the Costa del Sol, you can only exchange this for a similar period during the low season of properties elsewhere. Owners of the most expensive timeshare units have a much greater range of alternative resorts to choose from than those who buy the cheaper, off-season periods.

Some of the more popular destinations rule out off-peak customers altogether. For example, RCI advertises in its brochure three properties in central London where one might expect to pay £100 a night for a hotel room. All three are available for exchange only to people who have bought the most expensive timeshare units available. Exchanges are also restricted by availability; if the people who have bought the unit want to use it, clearly they have priority unless they have donated the time to a spacebank which will not happen so frequently at the most popular developments.

The RCI brochure rates the chances of availability from A, good, to E, very limited, and F, for new resorts where there is little chance of accommodation at all. Of the central London properties mentioned above, two are rated E and one D. In some areas, availability is extremely restricted. The six properties in Switzerland, for example, are all rated E or F, and availability tends to be restricted in most of Europe. Thus even with an expensive timeshare unit to exchange, your real choice may be limited.

The most obvious area for timeshare exchanges is in America, with easy availability listed for most of the resorts in the RCI brochure. However, the off-season for off-season rule applies, meaning, for example, that purchasers of a winter unit on the Costa del Sol may find themselves in ski resorts during snowless periods when few people want to use the accommodation. American resorts off-season can be distinctly more deserted than, say the Costa del Sol or the Canary Islands, where most Spanish timeshare is situated. Americans are increasingly interested in Spanish winter holidays, however, and may well snap up your Costa del Sol unit very rapidly, before you have the chance to find something acceptable in America. Under exchange rules, once you place your unit into the market it is up for 'sale' – and you cannot reclaim the booked unit you own even if you don't find anything you particularly like in the brochure.

Before counting exchange as one of the major bonuses of timeshare, it may be wise to look closely at the brochures of the exchange organisations and estimate how many other resorts you would *practically* expect to visit bearing in mind availability restrictions, cost of travel and the properties for which you might qualify. RCI had 120,000 European members in 1988 and arranged 68,000 exchanges on their behalf.

As well as arranging timeshare exchanges, organisations like RCI and II offer travel services such as flight booking, car hire and insurance. Prices for these services are competitive but rarely offer much in the way of savings when compared with the charges of High Street travel agents. In general, the charter flight prices in 1989 brochures were about on a par with those which the assiduous traveller could find elsewhere by ringing around several travel agents and tour operators. In some cases better fares and insurance quotes could be found elsewhere in what is a very competitive and fluid market.

There were some savings on Mediterranean scheduled fares which amounted to up to £40 a ticket on the equivalent available through travel agents and, for a family using these facilities, this could adequately pay the expenses of belonging to the exchange organisation. It is a moot point whether the membership fee of exchange organisations is justified by these added services.

THE DIFFERENT KINDS OF TIMESHARE

There are three principal kinds of timeshare contract, each of which has different implications for the purchaser. None is better or worse than another – but you should know which applies.

Freehold timeshare

This is fairly common in Spain, although impossible under English law. Purchasers genuinely own a share in the freehold of the development based upon the cost of their purchase. Freehold contracts are complex and can prove tortuous if a development runs into difficulties. They may also pose problems for anyone wanting to resell a timeshare unit.

Club membership

Increasingly the most popular option, club membership effectively makes the purchaser a member of a club which leases the property from the owner. The weeks of residence are the benefits which arise from belonging to the club. This is one of the simplest systems to administer and affords quick and problem-free resales.

Leasehold

Limited to the duration of the contract, which may be as little as 21 years. Some leasehold contracts may cause problems on resales: ensure that the contractual arrangement with the freeholder allows for the holder of the lease to sell it on to a third party.

The property world has a number of minor variations on these basic themes but, increasingly, you will find that new timeshare developments conform to one of these basic models, and that the contract will stipulate which. A member of the TDA (see p. 87) should provide you with a clear and understandable contract, in your own language, which answers all the points you need to know.

KEY QUESTIONS TO ASK

Many people are reluctant to involve a solicitor in a timeshare contract because they feel the sums involved do not warrant the payment of legal fees. As a general rule, I think it is only possible to purchase timeshare safely without taking formal legal advice if you are absolutely satisfied on two points:

— that you understand the nature and hidden costs of the contract being offered you and what commitments you will be taking on if you sign it

— that you are satisfied with the reliability of the developer/owner of the complex and his ability to deliver the services promised over a considerable period of years

Satisfaction on both these points means that you have considered the following aspects; it would be wise to take professional advice if you are uncertain on any of them.

1. The stature of the developer/owner

Timeshare complexes are frequently developed by a building company and the freehold then sold to a new owner. This may mean that you buy from one party and then pay maintenance to another. It is essential that you are satisfied that both companies are in a position to meet their obligations, and the best way to know that is by examining their standing and reputation in the field. One of the great risks in timeshare is that the freeholder will, over a period of years, find the complex does not produce sufficient return and, correspondingly, neglect some of the duties which he should fulfil in return for the maintenance which you pay him. In these circumstances it is extremely difficult indeed to force the freeholder to meet his obligations. Legal actions would be costly, protracted and difficult to pursue over a contract which affects only two weeks or so of the year.

The safest way to avoid these difficulties is to deal with a developer or owner of proven experience and long standing. Several well-known British companies, such as Wimpey and Costains, have Spanish timeshare developments and are less likely to default on their duties over the decades to come than a new company with no experience in the field.

In this sense buying timeshare is much like purchasing any leasehold property in Spain. You must always find out how long the seller has been in business, how many other developments he has built or currently owns, and then judge for yourself whether he is likely to deliver everything he promises.

This is particularly important in the case of units being sold on a development which is still under construction. Developers may start work on a complex, sell several units, and then go into liquidation before completion. In this case, purchasers may well find that their money will be taken by the bankrupt company's creditors, leaving them with nothing in return. This kind of event is rare, but by no means unknown. The best guarantee against it is to buy timeshare units, preferably in developments which have already been completed, through established companies with proven records and membership of the industry self-regulatory body. But do bear in mind that a familiar, British name does not save you from pressure selling. Indeed some of the worst offenders are High Street names in Britain.

2. Length of tenure

The period of tenure varies from contract to contract. Some stipulate a fixed period, for instance 30 years or occasionally only 21 years. Others grant occupation for life or even in perpetuity. A properly-worded contract in perpetuity forms part of your estate to be left in your will to your beneficiaries.

3. Cooling-off period

TDA members should allow purchasers a five-day 'cooling off' period during which they may return to the company and cancel the contract. Check that such a cooling-off period exists and whether you will be charged an 'administration fee' or some other penalty if you cancel within the period.

It is unwise to sign any timeshare contract which does not include any cooling-off period. This is normally one of the worst signs of high pressure selling and should be proof that the developer is not a member of the TDA.

4. Maintenance fees

All companies will charge you a maintenance fee. A good contract will set out very precisely in advance the extent of the fee and what it includes. You should expect maintenance fees to rise in line with inflation and it is preferable to have, in the contract, a clause which places a ceiling, say 15 per cent, above which they may not rise. Good timeshare developers will outline the schedule of the maintenance work included in the management fee – for instance, new furniture every six years, new central heating system every ten years, and so on.

The sums involved can add up to several hundred pounds annually and you will lose all rights to use and own the unit if you fail to pay them.

5. Consultation

Most timeshare developments will have some form of consultative organisation which liaises between the freeholder and the customers. This may be an annual general meeting or a customers' committee. In reality, given the nature of timeshare, such organisations are unlikely to be as effective as their equivalent bodies for property owners and full-time residents. However, it is important that the freeholders recognise the right of their customers to complain, even if it is scarcely feasible that many will be in a position to attend annual general meetings of timeshare owners. In some cases, pressure can lead to a change in the management company used by the freeholders to run the property.

6. Arbitration

Is there the option to go to independent arbitration to settle contractual and other disputes which may arise from the purchase? If there is not, then you will have to consult a lawyer to iron out any difficulties between you and the company which could prove expensive.

7. Rental

Does the property have a rental scheme? And if so, what commission does it charge for renting and how much are you likely to realise for your weeks if you do not use them?

8. Membership of an exchange organisation

As explained earlier, your chosen development must be affiliated to one of the large timeshare organisations, such as RCI or Intervals International, in order for you to be able to exchange your unit for holidays elsewhere in the world. You should find that membership details are clearly stated in the sales brochure, and often the first year's membership of the organisation is included in the sales fee for the unit.

If you are in any doubt whatsoever on these points when you look at the contract and talk to the developer's representatives, seek legal advice before signing any binding contract or handing over a deposit.

THE TIMESHARE DEVELOPERS ASSOCIATION (TDA)

The United Kingdom-based TDA was formed in 1987 in response to persistent Government suggestions that the industry had to introduce self-regulation of its activities or face the possibility of new statutory limitations on the ways in which timeshare is sold and run. The organisation represents about 60 per cent of British-owned timeshare companies. Since these are the principal developers of timeshare in Spain, it is not difficult to find a Spanish property which falls under TDA rules and guarantees about propriety and funding.

The TDA has been welcomed by the Government, although there remains some demand for a firmer stand against high pressure marketing practices and a tightening up of the rules for cooling-off periods. The TDA's code of conduct, while it does introduce some controls, still leaves plenty of scope for the kind of 'dynamic marketing' which has won timeshare its fair share of both critics and customers.

Control of marketing

The marketing guidelines allow, for instance, canvassing in public, though not in leisure areas, on condition that people are approached in a courteous way, without undue pressure, by a canvasser whose company is clearly identified. If you receive a written invitation, this should make it clear what it is you are being asked to participate in – so a timeshare sales pitch should not be disguised as something else. Nor, says the TDA, is it unreasonable to expect gifts from developers in return for time spent touring a resort, though the incentives should be clearly and accurately described before the visit. It is permissible for developers to make financial incentives to buy on the day, provided they are 'genuine'.

All TDA members must produce a clearly laid-out contract which you can cancel within a stated period – the minimum period allowed is five days – although you may have to pay a cancellation fee. So even a TDA canvasser may approach you on the street and try to entice you to see a timeshare unit with the offer of a free coach trip to Gibraltar, a bottle of champagne or several thousand pesetas... in return for which you could receive a pressure selling pitch which will offer you cash discounts in return for committing to buy the unit on the spot. These, remember, are the minimum standards imposed by 'responsible' timeshare companies.

'Buying timeshare you can trust'

The TDA's motto is 'Buying timeshare you can trust'. This is merited more by the organisation's insistence on financial and legal respectability among its members than its controls on marketing. All members must meet strict conditions regarding financial and business integrity, and prove the legality of their title deeds, timeshare documentation and resort management structures.

In addition, the TDA has introduced an independent arbitration service designed to settle disputes between timeshare customers and developers on a 'documents only' basis, without the need for solicitors. The scheme is based upon a similar complaints handling service introduced by the Association of British Travel Agents and the findings of arbitration are binding on member companies. In the first year of its operation, the TDA received 225 complaints about developments run by member companies throughout Europe. Like most such schemes, the end result is usually a compromise payment or change of contractual conditions which is, often grudgingly, agreeable to both parties.

Is the TDA worthwhile?

The guidelines of the TDA clearly leave something to be desired when it comes to controlling the sales techniques of timeshare developers. However, it *should* be the case that you can depend upon a TDA member to complete a timeshare development, run and maintain it properly, and offer you some form of guaranteed cooling-off period during which you may reassess your purchase. These guarantees, enforced by an independent arbitration service, make TDA properties clearly more attractive than rival schemes which fall under no regulatory body – at least in contractual terms.

FINDING TIMESHARE PROPERTY

So how *do* you go about tracking down a good timeshare property to which you will want to return year after year? A list of TDA-registered developments in Spain at the time of writing is included in the *Sources of Information* section at the end of this book. An updated list can be supplied by the TDA's offices. It would be unfair to suggest that only TDA members can supply you with good timeshare in Spain, however. Timeshare developments are advertised regularly in national newspapers and magazines, and appear in the displays of Spanish estate agents.

As with conventional property sales, it is far better to be your own master when finding an apartment or villa than to be at a developer's mercy. So, if you have the time, ignore the offers of cheap tickets for viewing flights, to be refunded if you buy, and make an independent visit to the area which interests you, window shopping and buying the local English language publications to track down potential developments. Timeshare developers are often surprised to discover potential customers who have sought *them* out, and you will find yourself instantly being regarded in a rather different light to those people who have been dragged in from the street.

Two final and important points about timeshare which are seldom appreciated. The salesman's display of discounts and incentives which accompany the closing of virtually every visit is part of a game which two may play. Timeshare prices, like all property prices, are open to negotiation, and there is nothing to stop you offering a lower price, in return for swift completion.

Lastly, you should never underestimate the persuasive powers of a timeshare sales team. They are professional, groomed in pressure selling techniques and working largely on commission. There is a very strong incentive for them to part you from your money and a battery of routines at their disposal to close the deal.

One simple precaution can foil most of these, however. *When visiting a timeshare complex, always, always leave your chequebook and credit cards safely in your hotel.* The offer of a taxi to reunite you with your money will be forthcoming, of course. But you will have achieved the first victory in dealing with timeshare pressure selling... leaving the development without having spent a penny.

7 Residency and Working

If you plan to spend any length of time in Spain each year, you should become aware of the rules governing residency and their associated financial implications. In the past, many people have drifted from being occasional visitor, to part-time resident and then to full-time residency. *Most* of these have managed to get away with breaking the country's residency rules.

However, the Spanish government is becoming increasingly efficient at enforcing residency regulations. If you are lax about counting the number of days spent in Spain, then you may one day count the price, which could result in being summarily expelled from the country. An increasing number of foreigners are being expelled each year. They are mainly young people without obvious means of support.

These rules will change for European citizens during the next decade, although they will doubtless continue to apply to everyone holding non-EEC passports. However, you should not assume that the harmonisation of EEC countries will guarantee free movement of labour and capital throughout Europe without any need for paperwork. Nor can you assume, as some people already have, that a possible liberalisation of work and residency regulations after 1992 will lead to infringements of the old rules being overlooked after this date. Changes in residency and work regulations may involve amnesties but they are rarely retrospective. If you are an illegal resident, working without a permit, you run the risk of being thrown out of the country and forbidden to return for three years.

There is no practical reason why most people should not live and work in Spain legally. Avoidance of the law is often more a case of impatience with the wheels of Spanish bureaucracy than an attempt to subvert the rules of the state. Understandable as this is, the risks are simply not worthwhile.

RESIDENCY REQUIREMENTS

When you visit Spain, you fall into one of three separate categories in the eyes of the official looking at your passport – as a tourist, a tourist on an extended visa, or a resident.

Tourist

You are a tourist if you spend less than six months of the year in Spain. The qualification is simply one of time not activity. You may own one or several properties or businesses in Spain, but, if your *total* time in the country does not exceed 183 days, then you are a tourist. Holders of EEC, USA and Japanese passports do not need a visa if their stay in Spain is for less than 90 days. If you want to stay longer as a preliminary to residency, you need a special visa, the *visado de residencia*, which can be issued by the Spanish Consulate. The requirements vary according to your status. A pensioner who does not intend to work will be asked for fewer details than someone who has been offered a job. If you wish to work, you will have to apply in person to the Spanish Consulate in London, fill in four forms, give details of the offer of employment, and supply, among other details, a medical certificate and four passport-sized photographs. One copy of the paperwork will then be sent to Spain for it to be registered with the employment authorities there. The applicant will be told when a decision is made – which may take several weeks – and will have to collect the visa personally. The cost is £36.

Whatever your intended status – employee, retired pensioner, or employer – do this before you leave Britain. Obtaining a *visado de residencia* is the normal preliminary to longer term residence; you apply to change your status when you get to Spain.

Turning up in Spain as an ordinary tourist, overstaying your 90 days illegally, and then trying to regularise the situation is a sure recipe for difficulties with the authorities. Nor is it advisable to try to fool the immigration desk by using up your 90 days, popping over the border to another country, and then coming back for a further 90 days as a tourist. You may get away with this, but legally you should still have a visa if you have spent in total more than 90 days of the year in Spain.

Tourist on extended visa

The *visado de residencia* is an extension of ordinary tourist status, often used as the first step to residency. Another form of 90-day extension offers a halfway house between tourist status and residency. It is available only once a year, so you may still not spend more than half the year in Spain as a non-resident. This is the *permanencia* which can be obtained at main police stations. You will need to show that you have sufficient funds to pay for your continued stay in Spain, usually with a bank statement.

The *permanencia* confirms tourist status on the holder. You can buy cars on 'tourist plates', saving on purchase tax. This is a popular way of saving money on new cars and you will find tax-free schemes advertised in all foreign language publications. The holder of a *permanencia* can also benefit from looser financial rules. He or she may move funds from currency to currency and country to country more easily than a resident. Many newcomers to Spain first obtain their *permanencia*, buy a property, and take on a new car on tourist plates at the same time. Then, you can apply for full residency in the knowledge that the investment in your property can be taken out of Spain again, and, thanks to tourist status, you have a tax-free car which can be used for five years in Spain as a resident.

Resident

If you know that you want to live in Spain for more than six months of the year, you should be planning to obtain a residency permit, the *autorización de residencia*. If you obtained a *visado de residencia* before leaving Britain, obtaining official residency should pose no problems, and you may apply as soon as you arrive.

The paperwork, and there is plenty of it, is best handled by a *gestor*. This is a peculiarly Spanish invention: a professional whose job is to steer the innocent's way through bureaucratic red tape. Your lawyer will be able to recommend a *gestor* or you will find their offices, *gestorías*, listed in phone directories. Prices vary from office to office, so shop around. The *gestor* will handle most of the bureaucratic tasks required in Spain, even property purchases, though the latter, as I have emphasised, are best left in the hands of a competent lawyer.

Obtaining your own residency permit will involve queueing in government offices and assembling a small mountain of paperwork. You should not attempt the task yourself unless you have a firm grasp of Spanish and plenty of time on your hands. You will need to produce a good deal of documentation about yourself, including a *certificado penal* which shows that you have no prison record in Spain, your *visado de residencia*, evidence of earnings, the signatures of two Spanish residents supporting your application, and photographs for the state records. The list can vary from office to office and according to whether you require a work permit at the same time. The only way to find out precisely what is required is to queue at the counter to ask, which is why the *gestor* is such a busy person.

Becoming resident makes you liable to Spanish laws on foreign exchange. The most important is the clause which forbids you to have an internal bank account in any currency other than normal pesetas. You may be given an exemption for this if your business requires it. One of the benefits of residence is that EEC residents become eligible for treatment under the Spanish state health service, though most continue to maintain a private insurance scheme.

Residence permits normally last for two years; renewal should simply be a formality. You can cease to be a resident just by handing in your permit to a police station. Residency is not the same as citizenship. To become a Spanish citizen you must fulfil stringent pre-conditions, one of them being residency in Spain for at least ten years.

For citizens of EEC countries there is little, if any, point in taking out Spanish citizenship; most foreigners living in Spain are Spanish residents but retain their original nationality. This allows them to retain their own passport but claim all the benefits of Spanish residency (and pay taxes just like the average Spanish citizen).

MOVING HOUSE

You will undoubtedly want to take some of your possessions with you when you move to Spain, and holiday home owners may well wish to furnish their purchase from Britain. There is a concession to those moving to take up residency in Spain. You are allowed to import all usual personal household possessions free of tax provided that they are at least six months old and you undertake not to sell them for two years. This concession is only available to those with a resident's permit. You can still take advantage of this concession if you have yet to obtain residency. You can apply for residency when you receive your initial *visado de residencia*. With proof of an application for residency, you will be allowed to import your possessions if you make a deposit of between 50 to 60 per cent of their value to the customs authorities. The deposit will be refunded when your residency is granted. There is a similar concession for holiday home owners but only if they do not let their property. Pets can be brought into Spain provided they have a range of medical certificates which have been stamped by the Spanish Consulate in your home country. The Consulate will provide up-to-date details on request; you should expect at least one certificate to be supplied only a matter of days before you depart.

Moving inevitably involves a lot of paperwork. However, there are a number of reputable international moving companies which will now do all the work for you, including arranging the tax free importation of your possessions. The best place to look for them is in the pages of *Lookout* magazine.

MOTORING

An international driving licence, issued by the RAC or AA on production of your own licence with photographs, allows you to drive in Spain for up to a year. An ordinary British driving licence is valid for six months. Many people illegally renew international permits year after year. To comply with the law, all residents must, after 12 months, obtain a Spanish driving licence. You will need a medical certificate and the services of a *gestor*. The process, which may take three months, consumes a high degree of paperwork, even by Spanish standards. You do not need to pass a new driving test unless your licence has lapsed or you are new to driving.

The business of owning a car in Spain is complex, since there are some rules by which foreigners can drive more advantageously than their Spanish neighbours. These exceptions are outlined briefly here, but they do require a fair amount of trouble and paperwork. There is a strong case for simply buying a car locally, duty paid in Spain. If you must take your beloved car with you, it is possible to export it from Britain to Spain free of duty provided that it has been used for six months and registered in your name before settling in Spain. This only applies to EEC citizens taking up permanent residency in Spain. It is legal to drive a British registered car in Spain for up to six months of the year. The figure is based on your time in the country – not the car's. If you spend five months in Spain and then bring in the car it may only be used for one month. At the end of the allowed period you have two choices. Either the customs authorities can 'seal' the vehicle, which means that they will effectively tell you not to use it until you wish to drive it out of the country again. Or you can register the car in Spain. This can be punitively expensive and complex, and is not recommended. Finally, you could sell the car, though it will not fetch much if it has run out of legal time on Spanish roads and is unregistered.

If you are an EEC citizen taking up residency, however, you can apply to import the car duty-free, in much the same way as furniture may be brought into the country. This is another job for the *gestor*, since it involves some intricate paperwork in reregistering the vehicle in Spain.

Many new residents buy cars on tourist plates, saving more than a third on list price by avoiding Spanish value added tax (IVA). You must buy the car, normally from a specialist dealer advertising in a tourist publication, when you are a tourist, normally awaiting residency. If you continue to live in Spain and bring in sufficient money from abroad to pay for your living costs, you may renew the tourist plates for up to four years. Dealers will normally handle the paperwork for you. If you are trying to earn a living locally your application for an extension of the plates will be refused. At the end of the four years, you can sell the car to another tourist who may then extend its use for a further four years... if he meets the right criteria.

Alternatively, you can buy a Spanish registered car. You will need a Spanish driving licence – which requires a residency permit – to drive the car so do not plan to buy locally immediately. There is an active second hand car market in the columns of local newspapers where you will find a familiar range of old bangers and reasonable runners. There is compulsory annual inspection of used vehicles much like the British MOT. Make sure that anything you intend to buy has its *inspección técnica de vehiculos*, the equivalent of an MOT. The transfer of the car to another owner is yet another task for a friendly *gestor*.

Road tax in Spain is charged locally and varies from area to area and according to the size of the vehicle. Third party insurance is compulsory, higher-rated third party or comprehensive cover advisable. Shop around from broker to broker to compare prices and cover just as you would at home. The overall cost of running a vehicle is comparable to that of Britain, though petrol is more expensive which steers cannier residents away from 'gas guzzlers'.

Most people with holiday homes in Spain either own a locally-bought and registered vehicle or drive their own car to their second home along one of the popular ferry routes. Car crime is rife in Spain; if you leave a vehicle at your villa unattended for some time do make sure that it is in a secure garage and inspected from time to time by a friend or helper.

WORKING IN SPAIN

No-one – not even the Spanish authorities, it seems – knows for certain how many foreigners live and work in Spain. The evidence of one's eyes reveals that Britons and other north Europeans are actively involved in enterprises large and small in all the popular resort areas, running a wide variety of enterprises from bars to restaurants, estate agencies to quick printing premises, public relations companies to building firms.

Many people have been beguiled into believing that working in Spain is some kind of guaranteed retirement to paradise. They have, perhaps, been fooled by that common stereotype of the Spanish male as an idle loafer, ever willing to dodge work and spending each afternoon in a long siesta after a substantial lunch.

Life is not like that, and for most people never was. The modern Spaniard works long hours with a good deal of dedication, and in some cities the siesta itself is beginning to disappear, with shops and other institutions opening throughout the afternoon until 8pm.

While the Spanish economy is improving and flourishing in some industrial sectors, unemployment remains high in many cities. Commercial life may move slowly in Spain, particularly when dealing with bureaucracies and state enterprises, but the average Spaniard is grateful to have a good job and will work hard to keep it.

If you want to make your way in Spain you will often need to accept the same long hours, middling wages and daily pressures which face the native worker and come to terms with a new language and way of doing business at the same time. Some of the toughest jobs are found in the very sector which most expatriates try to enter – tourism, which is extremely competitive and in some areas visibly over-supplied.

It remains a mystery where the stream of hopefuls ready to open 'genuine English-style pubs' in resorts like Torremolinos and Magalluf come from; there is, sadly, no secret about where most of them end up. Back home, many thousands of pounds poorer for their pains.

THE LEGAL FRAMEWORK

You cannot walk off a plane and straight into work in Spain, even if you are an EEC citizen. After 1992, the red tape should subside, and may even totally disappear. For the moment, you must expect to plan your move in advance, initially by contacting the Spanish Consulate for your *visado de residencia* and informing the authorities at this point that you wish to work in Spain. They will check out your job offer before issuing the visa.

Working for someone else mainly involves obtaining a work permit. If you wish to start your own business you will, in addition, face a veritable mountain of paperwork in Spain which varies according to the particular trade which interests you. This will involve checks on such things as whether you have a criminal record, are qualified for the work, and have the capital to begin the business.

Someone with good Spanish and the patience of a saint may be able to do this alone, but most people will employ a lawyer or *gestor* for the task. The latter, which is the cheaper option, might cost you £100 including official fees, and a lawyer double that. The cost is justified by the knowledge that the job has been done properly and you have been saved the time and trouble involved. There is not sufficient space here to outline the complete do-it-yourself process in full. If you require this kind of detail you will find it admirably conveyed in David Searl's book on Spanish law mentioned in the Bibliography.

Work permits

A work permit is necessary for everyone intending to work, except the self-employed or those who want to start a business, who need a different piece of paper. The work permit form is the same as the one with which you apply for residency. Before you can apply for the permit you must have obtained the *visado de residencia* from the Spanish Consulate in your home country. If you are a prospective employee, the authorities will ask themselves whether the job you have been offered could not be filled as well by one of the nation's own unemployed. If they think it could, they may well refuse your application. Specialist knowledge, bilingual abilities, and a technical background are the kinds of qualifications which the authorities smile upon.

A regular visitor to Spain will immediately point out that this fails to explain the presence in every coastal resort of a floating population of British bartenders, waiters and odd jobmen, many of whom are permanent residents. Well... Spain is a flexible country, it looks favourably upon employees who are relatives of the original owner of a business, and there is a handful of people who simply escape the net from year to year.

Work permits are initially valid for one year but may later be renewed every two years. People in temporary employment, tour company representatives and those irrepressible young people selling timeshare on the beach, for instance, can get temporary work permits for up to six months which are normally arranged directly by the employer.

Self employment and business owners

The piece of paper you require if you are an EEC citizen and want to work for yourself or run your own business is the *tarjeta comunitaria*. This is an EEC document which removes from this particular category of people the need for a *visado de residencia* and work permit. It does *not* mean that you will escape the attention of the Spanish bureaucrats. In order to get the *tarjeta* you must obtain a business licence, the *licencia fiscal*, from the tax authorities which allows you to set up your business. The criteria for the granting of the licence vary from profession to profession, and include the existing provision of the services you intend to offer in the region and your own professional experience.

In addition you will have to supply a certificate stating that you have no criminal convictions and register with the social security system as a self-employed worker. Social security payments of around £70 a month are lower for self-employed and business owners because they do not include provision for unemployment pay. It is possible to form a limited company to run the business. The commonest is the *Sociedad Anónima*, seen everywhere as the two letters *SA* at the end of company names. This offers the same kind of trading security and restraints as a limited company in the UK. Foreign investment in new Spanish companies must be agreed with the foreign exchange authority, the *Dirección General de Transacciones Exteriores*, and the company registered with a public notary. Companies with a large share capital, running into hundreds of thousands of pounds, may be told to raise some local participation in the project, but this may be negotiable. The assistance of a *gestor* or lawyer in these matters is desirable.

Employing other people

The authorities will look particularly favourably upon any application to start a business employing local labour. Whether you take on Spanish nationals as waiters or employ relatives in an office, you must register them with the social security offices and pay contributions which will amount to at least £100 per month per employee. A general calculation in Britain for the real cost of employees, including contributions, is to add a third to their basic salary. In Spain, the figure is more like 40 to 50 per cent, including the two annual bonuses, at Christmas and in July, which all workers will expect.

There are minimum conditions and special rules for different sectors of business. You should ask your adviser to explain what fixed holidays, overtime payments, and other entitlements will apply to employees in your particular venture, and to draw up a written contract for employees.

STARTING YOUR OWN BUSINESS

Some businesses prosper in Spain. Some fail miserably. What makes for a successful expatriate business? Perhaps the key factor is to make sure that the business you intend to run there is one which you know sufficiently well to succeed with back home. Spain does not turn bad chefs into good ones or transform the financially illiterate into stockbrokers. If you do not know how to do your job well at home, you will be just as ignorant in the sun, and there will doubtless be fewer people around willing to get you out of the mire.

Talk to those who have successfully translated their work there, however, and you will find two common threads running through every story. Most *knew* their line of work well before they ever came to Spain. And all have had to labour long and hard to achieve their goals.

The business plan

The various stages of setting up a business in Spain are similar to those required in Britain, but bear in mind the problems may be more daunting when you are without the familiar support system of banks and advisers speaking in your native language. Basic business research – the market you are aiming for, how much you need to make in order to live on – is essential. You must produce a sound business plan for your project, usually in association with your accountant. A business plan forces you to set down in writing precisely what you hope to achieve from your venture: its place in the market, its competition, how you intend to market the business, and the revenues and costs which you expect to face in your formative months and years. It is essential whether you are planning a small cocktail bar or a 300-seat restaurant and night club. Without it you will lack the parameters to detect which parts of your operation are meeting their targets and which are failing.

The creation of a business plan is well documented in business books and publications, and accountancy companies and banks will often provide leaflets to guide you through the process. The commonest mistake made in a business plan, and this is not confined to Spain although it can be more costly there, is to tailor your estimates of your income requirements to your forecasts of revenues and running costs. In plain language this means that you predict how much you are going to receive in income, deduct the costs of the business and then decide that you can live on the money that remains.

This way lies disaster. You should work from the opposite direction, making firm assessments of how much you need to take out of the business in order to live, based on local prices. And then see if you can meet your requirements from the revenues you predict. If you can't then the idea is fundamentally flawed unless you can somehow reduce your costs or increase your projected revenues.

Cheap drinks and restaurants often fool people into thinking that the cost of living in Spain is low generally. This was once the case but it is not so today. Spain has suffered a costly rate of inflation in the late 1980s and is paying the price of a large state bureaucracy. The cost of public services can be surprisingly high and clothing and household goods, to name just two commodities, are usually more expensive than in Britain. You should assume that your living costs will be roughly the same as they were before you moved.

Dealing with business agencies

'In 1984 Mr and Mrs Wilson from Doncaster, South Yorkshire, answered an advertisement by a British company in a British daily newspaper offering property and businesses for sale in Mallorca. They flew to Palma where, after being shown a number of properties by the British company's representative there, they decided to buy a seafront bar. The company's representative asked Mr and Mrs Wilson to pay a deposit of £3,500, being 10 per cent of the purchase price, into his account, which they did. Subsequently, they paid the balance, a further £33,000, to the company's representative in Spain. In June 1984 the company informed Mr and Mrs Wilson that the premises were now ready for occupation and so they wound up their affairs in England. On arriving in Mallorca they discovered that the bar premises were already occupied and operating as a fast food bar. The company's representative said that he had invested the Wilsons' money in a different property which was a better investment, although more expensive. They reluctantly accepted his explanation and agreed to make a further transfer to his account.

However, work on the second property failed to advance and the Wilsons were informed by a Spanish lawyer that the contract for the purchase of the second property was worthless and fraudulent. He advised them to sue the English company in English law for the return of the monies so far paid out.

In December 1984, the Wilsons obtained a court judgment ordering the English company to repay £42,500, but they did not receive the money as the company went into liquidation in January 1985. The company's managing director has, they say, since formed a new company and continues, it is understood, to trade in Spanish property.'

This salutary tale from Edward McMillan-Scott's report to the European Parliament is unusual but not unique. Financial difficulties and, on occasion, outright fraud are no strangers to commercial transactions everywhere, and Spain is no exception. Nor can they be avoided simply by dealing with British organisations, as the story above demonstrates.

Most agencies dealing in business transfers are honest and reliable. They work on much the same commission terms as estate agents, and a number of estate agents also deal in business transfers. Even so, you *must* obtain professional advice, from a lawyer or accountant, both to ensure the legality of the transaction and to establish your own book-keeping practices so that they can satisfy Spanish taxation regulations covering matters such as value added tax (IVA).

One of the commonest causes of problems in buying and selling businesses is the matter of the *traspaso*, the lease for the premises concerned. Sometimes, the *traspaso* being offered by an agency is being sold on behalf of the tenant of the premises, without the knowledge of the owner. There may well be a clause in the contract which forbids this and allows the owner to step in and institute a new, higher rent or force out the latest occupant.

In one case on the Costa del Sol, an unsuspecting bar owner was expelled from his premises after a year in business because it turned out that his *traspaso* had been passed on over several years by several different holders of the lease before him. By the time the owner of the property discovered that the occupier of his premises was far removed from the legal holder of the lease, the original tenant was back in Britain, well away from the financial agonies he had caused to several innocent parties in Spain.

Business agents may have a wide selection of ventures on their books, but most will be bars, restaurants or shops in tourist areas. You will often be supplied with turnover figures by the selling agents. Take them with a pinch of salt unless your adviser indicates otherwise. Turnover, even if it is accurate, is a very vague indication of what you might be able to produce from the business. Remember that agents are always working on a commission. As with property transactions, you will save money by locating what you want personally, visiting during business hours to get a more accurate picture of the true level of custom and making an offer direct. The owners of small businesses in Spain are not shy when it comes to letting the world know that they are open to offers. A sign reading *Se Traspaso* or for rent may appear on the shopfront, or you can quickly pick up the gossip in a neighbourhood bar or wherever the expatriate community meets.

Finding your own business is more time-consuming than using agents, but you should save money and be able to view what is on offer dispassionately, without the sales pitch.

New apartment developments often include bare shells for commercial use, and resorts invariably have several purpose-built units. These identical breeze block skeletons are ingeniously transformed each season into some new business. Always try to discover what purpose neighbouring units are to be put to, since this avoids the embarrassing discovery that you are the ninth genuine English steak bar in a row in the same development. Leases for new premises may seem inexpensive but this is often deceptive. You should budget for the conversion of the shell into whatever you require, and the purchase of all the working fittings you will need. Normally the furnishing, and occasionally stock, of existing businesses will be included in the purchase price.

You do not need to understand the legal complexities of leasing business property. Nor should you waste time trying to comprehend these matters. Concentrate on the practical side of setting up the business – work permits, funding and finding staff – and leave legal matters to your professional adviser. Never, never pay any money to any party, however forceful the demand or threat of losing the deal, except when instructed by your professional adviser.

WHAT TYPE OF BUSINESS?

There is no practical or legal limitation on the kind of work which you can pursue in Spain. Some, mainly those in the financial world who can survive on a fax machine and a computer link, manage to carry on the same business which they ran in their home country. Most people work in catering, in tourist-related industries, run business service companies, or use their professional qualifications to set up as consultants.

Catering

The commonest type of business available through agents marketing 'opportunities' in tourist Spain is a bar or restaurant available on a lease. Some people have made good livings out of running a catering establishment in Spain. It could be a 'Bull and Bush' style pub selling steak and kidney pie and chips in

Torremolinos or an upmarket restaurant serving international cuisine in Marbella.

Be under no illusions: *no other market is so hard for the newcomer to Spain to enter successfully, even with relevant experience.*

Why? The degree of skill required to become a successful restaurateur or pub landlord is widely undervalued. Catering is about more than cookery, running a pub goes beyond pulling pints. Many catering ventures in Britain fail because those behind them fail to appreciate these simple truths. In a foreign environment, the risk of failure is even greater.

Some catering or licensing trade experience is advisable for anyone planning to open such a business. Having said that, a number of complete beginners have opened bars in tourist resorts and some, principally through the force of their personality and an innate marketing skill, have done well. Spanish drinks companies have tailored their services to meet this unskilled sector of the market and will now handle all the technical side of running a bar, right down to cleaning the beer pumps.

The greatest threat to the new entrant in the Spanish catering business is the state of the market; by any yardstick most popular resort areas have far more bars and restaurants than can possibly be supported by the local population, resident and transient. Except for the peak of the season, competition is fierce, profit margins low, and business tenuous.

Working hours are longer than most people would consider acceptable in Britain. Many English-owned bars will open at 9am to serve breakfast and continue to serve drinks until 2am or 3am, often seven days a week during the peak of the season. Restaurants match Spanish eating hours, serving meals until well past midnight.

Most foreign owners of catering establishments spend the greater part of their days on their premises. Few have enough free time to explore the part of the world where they have chosen to live. The pressures on family life which accompany all catering businesses are intensified in Spain by a foreign environment and the long working hours necessary to maintain the momentum of the business.

The personalities and experience of the owners apart, one of the principal commercial factors which decides the success or failure of a catering establishment in a coastal resort is location. Those sited close to the centre of the resort or large hotels or villa complexes invariably fare better than identical bars or restaurants in more out-of-the-way locations. Every resort has more than its fair share of premises which will *never* become viable because of their very inaccessibility, and one can watch them change hands year after year as some new hopeful takes over the reins.

The only establishments which can successfully force their customers to come to them are those which have a particular attraction, often aimed more for the resident foreign population than the transient holidaymaker. It may be expensive French cuisine, a Vietnamese chef, or the best jazz band on the coast. There is no substitute for personal observation for anyone contemplating opening a catering business in Spain. Visit existing premises, preferably at peak and low periods, and try to work out for yourself what differentiates the busy from the quiet. You will find the owners ready to talk about their successes and their problems, even to potential competitors. Judge for yourself how hard it is to stand out from the crowd of premises fighting for the customer's eye. And think very hard before committing yourself to joining a battle in which the losers outnumber the winners several times over.

Tourist retailing

After catering, the most common form of business to be found on the market in tourist areas is the small resort shop selling newspapers, beach items and small gifts. Many are family-run enterprises – whether English or Spanish. The same economic considerations which affect catering establishments apply. Geographic location is normally the key to turnover. Shops close to the beach and resort hotels have a ready, captive clientele, and invariably cost more than those which are harder to reach. The former may be the only viable units to lease. You can find out by comparing their claimed turnover with that of an unfavourably located shop. Does the added trade pay for the extra premium on the price? And even if it doesn't, is there sufficient money in the smaller business to pay your way? Why *are* the present owners selling, and how long have they been in business there?

...me experience in the retail trade is invaluable. You will need to monitor stock levels of a large number of items and set profit margins which give you sufficient return. If retailing is new to you, talk to an accountant about the likely cash flow of the business. Retailing in many areas is seasonal, and it may not be worthwhile opening the shop during the winter. Shop opening hours are not as punishing as those of catering but are still longer than those generally worked in the UK. In season a well-situated shop should expect to open around 9am and close between 8pm and 9pm seven days a week. The actual working hours are often longer, of course, since book-keeping and stocktaking can be undertaken only when the premises are closed.

Service companies

Bars, restaurants and shops come and go. The people who service them, and the population as a whole, stay around much longer. Some of the smartest expatriate businessmen and women in Spain are those who have spotted the need for some service on the part of the community and set themselves up as the company to provide it... swimming pools installed by British workmen, the manufacture of English or German style sausages and pies, printing, publicity and promotional facilities for that army of new restaurateurs which needs to publicise itself every spring.

If you can define a need in the community and fill that niche you will create for yourself a new business which may be more profitable than more obvious opportunities and, in the end, less work. The small army of enterprising expatriate businessmen and women in Spain are easy to spot while house-hunting.

The professions

Professional people – doctors, lawyers, accountants and others who need set qualifications in order to practise – are in a difficult position at the time of writing. In order to practise in Spain, they must obtain local qualifications in addition to those which they have gained in their home country. This is a considerable disincentive to many potential applicants, though a growing number of professionals now take the time to qualify in Spain in addition to their existing credentials. The size of the expatriate population means that there is a ready market for the services of people from a customer's own country.

These restrictions *should* change for EEC citizens in 1992. The provisional arrangements for professionals who are citizens of the EEC are that they will be allowed to practise in other countries after a short induction period during which they will be introduced to the relevant practices of the new country. They will not, as they must do at present, be forced to join the relevant Spanish professional organisation.

You may care to judge for yourself how practical this might be for different professions. A doctor, for instance, is dealing with very much the same creature wherever he works in the world, and may be better equipped to deal with people in his native language. But which would you prefer as a lawyer – someone with local and British qualifications or a newcomer with impeccable British qualifications but no direct, certified training in Spanish law? Until 1992 this remains a matter of conjecture.

WORKING FOR SOMEONE ELSE

Unemployment is high in Spain and most job vacancies are taken up by native workers. Temporary work, sometimes illegal, can be found in some foreign-owned bars and restaurants, though the penalties can be unfortunate if you are caught. Timeshare companies will, legally, employ young people on temporary contracts as sales representatives normally working on a commission basis.

You should not expect to take a full-time, legal post which could adequately be filled by local labour. In order to enter the jobs market, you need some extra qualification which will attract an employer... and the contract which will get you a work permit. There is no common labour exchange which advertises vacancies. You will need to track down the jobs for yourself, through the columns of local newspapers or personal visits to resorts as a tourist.

What do employers look for? Perhaps the first question asked by a manager looking to fill a serious post is why you are there in the first place. Do you have a positive reason for being in

Spain rather than Britain, or are you simply in search of a pleasurable lifestyle? How good an employee were you in Britain? Do you have any references that he could take up or, even better, a letter from a former employer vouching for your reliability?

You can help yourself by providing your own well-presented curriculum vitae, preferably with written references from people you have worked for in the past. Always remember that the labour market in Spain works to the advantage of the buyer. Your potential employer has any number of local people who would like the vacancy he has to offer. You need to present something extra... such as some kind of job experience from Britain which will be valuable and hard to find in Spain. Fluency in Spanish, preferably written and spoken, will open many doors for you. Not simply because the linguistic ability will be useful, but also as proof of the effort you are willing to make to find work in a new country.

Finally, don't knock Britain in the interview – try to concentrate on the positive aspects of your interest in Spain. Your interviewer will have heard every expatriate gripe in the book, and be unamused to have them retold again. If a job offer does materialise, make sure you receive a written contract which will be necessary to obtain a work permit. Do not accept verbal job offers 'on trust'. This usually means that you are expected to work illegally without a contract enforceable in law.

Tour companies

The package holiday business is labour intensive. Becoming one of the many tour reps working in the large resorts can be a useful way to learn about working in Spain. The Thomson group, Britain's largest tour operator, alone employs more than 2,000 people in Spain each year as overseas representatives and children's representatives.

The job of a package tour rep is extremely hard work. There are no fixed hours, a holidaymaker's life is often full of problems, and the pay is relatively low. But the popularity of the job means that tour companies can fill most of their vacancies from the letters they receive without having to advertise for applicants. A tour rep's life will involve dealing with Spanish businesses and learning Spanish; many people now working full-time in resort-based businesses from estate agencies to public relations consultancies began their careers in Spain guiding package holidaymakers from the airport to their hotel.

Thomson's job requirements are fairly standard for the industry. They start to consider applicants each September and aim to bring in new recruits in April, after a one-week intensive training course. The workforce halves each winter, but those requiring year-round work can usually find it. Thomson does not demand knowledge of Spanish from applicants to be overseas representatives, but they must speak two European languages and learn Spanish when they take up work. Overseas representatives must be over 21. No set qualifications are demanded, but the successful candidates will have 'personality, a good sense of humour, and be willing to work the hours needed to keep holidaymakers happy', the company says. Children's representatives must be over 18 and have some kind of childcare qualification.

8 Arranging your Finances

Money matters should always be in the mind of anyone thinking of spending some time abroad. How do you arrange your tax affairs so that you pay as little as legally possible, and to whom do you pay tax? What is the best way to guarantee a return on an investment? How do you make sure that the local taxes on a property are paid when you are not always there? And these questions are multiplied many times for anyone thinking of starting a business.

Mistakes can be costly and difficult to rectify. Many retired people on the Costa del Sol are now paying dearly for using the wrong financial investment company. They were customers of the Barlow Clowes finance house subsidiary in Gibraltar which failed in 1988, along with the rest of the empire. Many lost their life savings and the monthly interest which was their principal income. Because they used the Gibraltar arm of the company, they have, to date, failed to receive even the modest amount of compensation which has been awarded to investors in the company who used UK financial advisers.

Ironically, Barlow Clowes had a public face which seemed to guarantee security and distance it from the companies offering impossibly high returns. Barlow Clowes offered relatively low interest on deposits and did so, it claimed, because it concentrated only on the safer portfolios. The truth, as we now know, was that the company took high risks *and* paid low returns. With the benefit of hindsight, it is easy to say that those who invested in Barlow Clowes might have chosen better. But many were recommended by professional investment advisers who should have been forewarned of problems with the group's trading.

Fortunately, the position over investment advisers is now somewhat clearer, if you go about selecting your financial consultant in the right way.

SEEKING FINANCIAL ADVICE

A financial adviser will offer a wide range of services, from life assurance to mortgages, offshore funds to health insurance schemes. A good adviser can save you a great deal of money; a bad one can lose you everything.

FIMBRA

The Financial Services Act of 1988 introduced self-regulation to the financial services industry and brought a new measure of security to the private investor. The regulatory body is the Financial Intermediaries, Managers and Brokers Regulatory Association (FIMBRA) which imposes a strict code of conduct on members and the way they deal with the public.

The Financial Services Act is in force in the United Kingdom *and* the Channel Islands. So if you conduct offshore business with a member on Jersey you will be covered by its regulations. It does *not* have any force in Spain, even with subsidiaries of companies which are FIMBRA members in Britain. For instance, a bank selling financial services to the public in the UK must be a FIMBRA member, but its Spanish branch need not be and can work outside the FIMBRA rulebook.

In the case of a large and well-known clearing bank, the difference may be notional – it isn't going to run away with your money when the financial going gets tough. Things might be different with subsidiaries of smaller investment companies which do not have the spread of interests of a large clearing bank. Some investors affected by the Barlow Clowes collapse did place their money through Spanish subsidiaries of FIMBRA companies. If they had done so in Britain, they would have received some compensation and the company responsible for the investment would have had its knuckles rapped by the regulatory body. In Spain, there is no such redress, as a lot of very unhappy investors, most from the UK, have discovered to their cost in recent years.

Financial advisers should be chosen with the utmost care. While FIMBRA membership of a UK head office may not bring the direct benefits of FIMBRA cover to Spanish branches, it is an indication that the parent institution has managed to pass some fairly rigorous investigations of its procedures and stature.

INVESTMENT

The criteria involved in choosing how to invest money are the same in Spain as anywhere else. Generally speaking, investments either result in a high return, with a correspondingly greater risk of losses, or a modest rate of interest but with absolute security. The route you choose will be determined by how much money you have available, how much you need to take out quickly as income, and how important it is to guarantee your original investment. There is no simple solution in these matters, and many people will opt for a combination investment strategy, placing part of their savings in schemes which produce a regular monthly sum year in year out and the remainder in a more speculative portfolio designed to produce returns above the rate of inflation.

The financial world in Spain is not as closely regulated as that of Britain, and there are several small finance houses operating, particularly on the Costa del Sol, which would have a hard time obtaining permission to open offices in Britain. They make a living out of selling investment schemes promising high returns to gullible expatriates, most of whom end up disappointed. Being able to advertise in a local publication is no guarantee of financial health. Wherever possible deal with companies which have been personally recommended or are part of a large, well-known group.

All the major banking institutions in Britain run schemes designed for the expatriate. Most have offices in the Channel Islands which run high interest rate, tax-free schemes offering income, growth or a combination or both. Expatriates may also hold interest-bearing accounts with UK bank offices and have earnings paid without the deduction of tax which is applied to deposit accounts for UK residents.

The rewards of sticking with the proven names may never be as spectacular as you might get from a maverick new finance house with a nose for worldwide bargains. But you won't lose any sleep at night worrying where your money is. There is nothing wrong with a gamble on shares...so long as you understand that it *is* a gamble, full of attendant risks.

Every individual situation is different. You should always bear in mind that financial investments which are geared to the share market do involve risks. Prices can rise and fall, and a good investment consultant will emphasise this when discussing your financial affairs.

Offshore funds

If you are planning to live in Spain, and inform the British tax authorities that you are no longer a UK resident, you will become eligible to invest in specialist expatriate offshore funds. These are legally-sanctioned investment schemes designed to provide a high degree of return. They are managed by both major and minor institutions.

Funds are share portfolios – a combination of holdings in a range of companies. The breadth of the portfolio is meant to cushion you from the ill effects of one member company's poor results. By spreading the risk, the argument runs, you minimise the chances of nasty shocks. This is true, but never forget that share portfolios remain linked to the international stock market and, as such, can never simply be a source of guaranteed income for those who indulge in them.

Managed funds may specialise in a particular industry or geographical region, high technology or Japan, for example. Or else they could cover a broad field of industrial and commercial companies. Do not become too exposed in specialist areas unless you are sure of what you are doing.

A specialist adviser should be able to give you an indication of the risk ratio of different kinds of investment. If he or she is a member of FIMBRA, then such advice *must* be offered. You cannot be pressed to take one particular fund simply because the adviser is being offered a good commission for selling it.

Offshore funds may be based in any of the many centres which specialise in such services, such as the Channel Islands, the Cayman Islands, or Bermuda. Gibraltar is a popular base for both large and small funds. But your dealings with the fund will usually be through a broker, so there is no significant advantage in choosing one which happens to be near to Spain.

TAXATION

Spain is not a tax haven. It is difficult and unwise to try to avoid paying taxes on income and property imposed by the tax authority, Hacienda. Nor is Spain a low-tax country. If you become resident and start a business you may find that you are paying just as much tax as you did in Britain. Finding good financial advice so that you avoid problems with the tax authorities is as important as using a lawyer for property purchase.

Income taxes

Anyone who spends more than 183 days of the year in Spain is liable to pay income tax to Hacienda on *all* his or her income, wherever in the world it was earned. To the authorities, you are just another Spanish taxpayer. If you spend less than 183 days in Spain but have income within the country then you are liable to be taxed on that income. The taxation system is currently undergoing reform, so there is little point in outlining here specific tax rates which will doubtless change. The Spanish Consulate or a financial adviser will be able to provide an up-to-date breakdown of current tax rates. The general levels of taxation in Spain are comparable with those in Britain. Tax contributions by employed people are normally deducted from the monthly pay packet, some self-employed people may make quarterly payments, and others will pay with the settlement of their annual return.

No-one earning under a set limit, 840,000 pesetas per annum at the time of writing, pays tax. A number of allowances, such as a marriage allowance and travelling expenses to work, can be set against the annual tax bill.

In addition to income tax, you will have to pay a tax on your assets, the *impuesto extraordinario sobre el patrimonio*. This is currently one fifth of a percent, levied against an individual's assets, usually their property. Many people owning only one home fall below the limit at which the tax becomes payable and consequently are charged nothing. The tax is essentially a means of enabling the state authorities to keep track of asset ownership, not, at the moment, a source of substantial tax revenue.

Holiday home owners, spending fewer than 183 days in Spain, are still liable to both income and asset tax. The income tax will apply to any money they have earned in Spain, from property rental or any other activity. Asset tax too must be paid on the basis of the value of assets in Spain.

Double taxation

Spain has what is known as a double taxation agreement with Britain and many other countries. In spite of its rather threatening name, a double taxation agreement is designed to help you pay less tax, not more. It applies when you are taxed by two countries on the same income. Britons face the situation when they first move to Spain. The British taxman will not regard them as expatriates beyond his reach until they have been abroad for a full tax year. However, the Spanish will be demanding tax once they have stayed more than 184 days.

A double taxation agreement allows you to set the Spanish tax charge against the UK demand. In order to do so you will need to produce a form proving that you have paid the tax in Spain. Inland Revenue offices will supply the necessary documentation and explain the system in more detail if necessary. The calculation can become complex if you have any savings which have been taxed at source, and for people owning shares and Government stock. An accountant or financial adviser may be needed to help you claim partial or full exemption in these cases.

Dealing with the tax authorities

Tax returns are normally filed with Hacienda once a year, at the time of writing in May and June, and the amount due will be paid during these months. Late and inaccurate returns can attract heavy fines. Many foreign residents with simple tax affairs have learnt, over the years, how to deal with the annual return to Hacienda. The paperwork involved is no more difficult – or simple – to complete than a British Inland Revenue annual return. You will be asked to disclose all income, including bank deposit accounts. All available allowances can then be set against the income and the tax due assessed on the current rates. Hacienda employs staff to answer public inquiries and advise on filling in returns, though they will not do the work for you. Newcomers, who will in most cases be employing an accountant for other reasons, are advised to leave the matter in the hands of a professional and perhaps take the cheaper option of using a *gestor* in later years before handling all the task privately.

Municipal taxes

The Spanish equivalent of domestic rates is the *contribución urbana* which is fixed by the local town hall and charged to owners of all private properties. You may also discover that there are small local taxes for rubbish or sewage disposal in some areas. Municipal taxes cause holiday home owners in particular a great deal of trouble. Demands may be sent to owners' homes in Britain when they are actually occupying their holiday villa, or arrive some weeks after the deadline for payment has expired. Some properties to the author's knowledge on the Costa del Sol have, through some clerical error, failed to be charged rubbish dues for several years, and the money has been refused by the local authority when it has been offered by bemused residents.

The problem with these relatively modest municipal taxes is that non-payment is always met with a surcharge and *nothing* , certainly not incompetence on the part of the public authority, is accepted as an excuse for failing to pay a bill. Small demands which are bumped up by 20 to 40 per cent through non-payment can soon become rather large. The simplest way to guarantee payment of regular demands is to authorise your bank to pay them on demand whenever possible.

BANKING

The type of bank accounts which you use in Spain will depend upon your status. Non-residents may only open three kinds of accounts: non-resident convertible currency accounts, non-resident convertible peseta accounts, and non-resident ordinary peseta accounts. The first two are the more flexible. There are no restrictions on transfers from abroad or transfers out of the country except that currency notes can only be credited if the importation of the money has been declared to the customs authorities. Credits to these accounts from within Spain can only come from another non-resident account or money earned in special circumstances set out in the taxation laws. You are not allowed to place the income from renting property into a convertible account.

The non-resident ordinary peseta account is effectively an ordinary Spanish bank peseta account. Money in it cannot be transferred abroad, and if you move money from your convertible account into it then it ceases to be exportable. Peseta accounts are normally used for paying the everyday bills of holiday homeowners.

Residents normally run everyday Spanish cheque accounts, which usually bear interest. Foreign exchange regulations will restrict how much you can take out of this account and move abroad. It will be enough for a foreign holiday, but you will not be allowed to shift large sums of money out of the country. This should change in 1992 for EEC citizens moving deposits into other EEC countries. All the usual services of modern western banking, from standing orders to cash and credit cards, are available from Spanish banks. A number of British banks now have subsidiaries and branches in Spain. There is much to be said for placing all of one's financial transactions – bank accounts, mortgages, health insurance and investment – in the hands of a trusty UK clearing bank well represented in Spain. You will find a list of the ones in tourist areas listed on pp.138-40.

9 Everyday Life

After the giant steps of buying property and working through the bureaucracy of Spanish immigration rules lie the everyday chores – such as getting the phone connected, finding schools, and sorting out satisfactory health arrangements. Spain is a modern European nation – virtually any service which you might expect to find in Britain can also be supplied in your new home, probably at a similar price and quality whether it is a supply of shrubs from the local garden centre or a filling by the neighbourhood dentist.

In areas popular with foreign residents, the local commercial community has adapted itself to the tastes and requirements of its new, free-spending neighbours. Satellite dishes to receive foreign language television channels, swimming pool companies offering installation by British workmen, and supermarkets selling Danish bacon, Heinz baked beans and Cornish pasties – locally made – are busy serving the expatriate colony. British and north European doctors, specialists and dentists offer private medical services to customers who prefer to be treated by someone from their own country.

In out-of-the-way areas the story is different. Medical and educational services are as restricted as their counterparts in British rural areas. Many remote rural homes on the market do not have basic services and it can be expensive and time-consuming to connect them. It is possible to install an electrical generator, solar heating equipment, gas tanks and a water collection system as an alternative, but the costs may be substantial. These factors are all part of the price of living in rural Spain and must be assessed at the time of purchase.

Water can be a serious problem in many areas, particularly in small villages with temporary summer holiday populations. Additional drinking water may have to be brought in by tanker at extra cost to maintain supplies during the peak of summer. This can lead to periods of rationing or complete loss of supplies. Similarly, there may be a limited collection of household rubbish by the local authority, or none at all, a rural problem seen everywhere which leads to illegal dumping and burning of waste.

Talk to local people in the village to assess the situation – you will often find that water and rubbish disposal hold the place in everyday Spanish conversation that the weather does for the British. Sewage disposal may be primitive or even non-existent in rural homes which, at a passing glance, may seem idyllic. Even some palatial rural homes continue to use drain-away sewage systems identical to those of two centuries ago.

Urban areas usually have adequate facilities for disposal of household waste through the ubiquitous black bag, the *basura*, but larger items may need to be taken to a municipal dump. Rubbish collection hours in Spain are flexible, and in some resorts the dustbin men have an unnerving habit of doing their rounds in the early hours of the morning. Water and drainage facilities in most urban areas are competent if occasionally somewhat amateurishly constructed. Efforts are being made in many coastal areas to do away with the pumping of untreated sewage into the sea, under pressure from both the EEC and vociferous holidaymakers. Industrial pollution remains a problem along many parts of the coast, however. The Mediterranean is, of course, polluted for much of its length, and Spain is no better or worse than any other nation. It may not have the horrors of the Bay of Naples, but care should be taken about bathing in industrial areas.

Spanish drinking water is, in almost all urban areas, perfectly safe to drink. It usually tastes unpleasant, however, and most residents follow the example of the Spanish and drink bottled, uncarbonated mineral water which is cheap, of good quality and available at every corner shop.

The main point to remember about all public services in Spain is that they may take a long time to materialise for properties which do not already have them. A new telephone line may involve a wait of up to a year. Power may not be connected to a new estate until every last house is built – and may never come if the *urbanización* was built without planning permission.

If your home has services already installed, then it should simply be a matter of taking them over and informing the relevant authorities of the change of ownership. You may find a few small bills outstanding from the previous owner, partly due to the slowness of Spanish authorities in sending out invoices.

Bottled gas, readily available, is cheap and commonly used for cooking and heating. Solar heating and heat pump systems are installed in many foreign homes in tourist areas. These are expensive to buy, but should make for inexpensive heating for many years if they are installed properly. Both systems really only make financial sense for people who are going to live in Spain for most of the year. Beware any salesman who tries to convince you that solar heating will supply *all* your home's energy requirements. A more realistic assessment is that it will heat water and a swimming pool to acceptable levels. Heat pump systems may also require back-up heating systems for temperatures below 5°C.

Electricity is 220 volts or 225 volts AC almost everywhere, although some buildings still have 110 volts or 125 volts AC. Two-pin plugs are standard. Most UK household electrical equipment will run adequately on 220 volts or 225 volts AC when fitted with new plugs, though some equipment may need to be earthed. If in doubt, contact the manufacturer or seek advice from a local electrician. The Spanish television standard differs from Britain. British-bought television sets and video recorders will need to be replaced.

EDUCATION

Your children can take standard UK GCSE exams, attend an English-style prep school, or become part of the Spanish state education system. The choice is yours. Many expatriates do now place their children in Spanish schools. There is no charge and many have a reasonable academic reputation, although some parents accuse them of concentrating too much on learning by rote instead of teaching creatively.

Important factors in the decision will be the age of the child and whether you intend to return to England. A young English-speaking child of nursery or early infant school age will quickly pick up Spanish in classes and may well develop more bilingual abilities than his parents in a remarkably short time. Mastery of English and Spanish enables the boy or girl to move easily between expatriate and local communities and will stand the child in good stead in a multi-lingual Europe.

There is no reason why this linguistic ability cannot be encouraged at an early age, and the child then moved to an international school later to take GCSE exams. The two educational systems are not mutually exclusive.

Older children will undoubtedly suffer some difficulties when thrust into the Spanish system without a good grasp of the language or the different classroom practices. This may set them back a year in the educational stream for linguistic reasons alone. These problems may arrive at an age when the child is aware of the friends left behind in Britain for the new life in Spain, exerting more stress on family relationships.

Many older children do adapt to Spanish schools in this way and catch up but it can be a difficult process and one which a large number of parents would prefer to avoid, particularly if they feel that the children will eventually want to return to Britain. Private tutoring in Spanish is advisable and can be located through local newspaper advertisements. In rural areas and towns outside the tourist regions there will rarely be any choice apart from Spanish state or church schools.

Once again, personal recommendation is the best way to to find the best school. International and private Spanish schools may be visited before placing children to discuss classroom attitudes and curricula and inspect educational and sporting facilities (which vary widely). One final option, which continues to be popular with many of the wealthier parents in Spain, is to board children at established British or European schools and arrange visits during holidays.

International schools

A list of international schools in Spain which can teach to UK curricula is included in the appendix, with average costs per year and the age range of pupils. This is provided by the European Council of International Schools for information purposes, not for recommendation. International schools in Spain are not limited to British curricula, however. American, French and German schools also exist and are listed by the ECIS. Some will offer a dual system of Spanish and native language qualifications which, with the right choices, can ensure that the child is equally well qualified to live and work in Spain or in his or her mother country when older.

This 'mix and match' approach to the curriculum can prove very attractive for people who want to keep open all options for the future.

There is no league table of educational achievement for Spanish schools, but, within the expatriate community, there is a firm belief that good international establishments are more likely to lead to places at British universities than Spanish schools, if only because the qualifications gained by pupils are better known to the selection bodies.

Spanish schools

There are three basic types of Spanish school – those run by the state, private schools, and those run by the Catholic Church. State schools are free and may be attended by all children resident in Spain. Private and church schools charge fees but these are usually modest since they also receive a subsidy from the state. There is no insistence on religious studies in state schools; students may take an ethics course instead. Naturally, church schools will have a Catholic background which normally makes religious studies obligatory. School education is compulsory for all children aged between six and 16 years.

Pre-school education

Voluntary pre-school education is available in state and private facilities. State pre-school classes are free; private schools charge, the more expensive being the unsubsidised international schools. Spanish pre-school education is divided into two levels. The *Jardín de Infancia* is for children aged two and three, and the *Escuela de Párvulos* for four and five-year-olds. There has been a rapid growth in state pre-school facilities in recent years, from under 900,000 places in 1970-71 to 1,127,348 in 1985-86. However, there are strong regional variations in provision. You will need to find out for yourself what facilities, if any, exist in the area which interests you.

Educación General Básica

The core of the compulsory education syllabus is the EGB, General Basic Education, which is the basis of classes in both state and private schools. EGB is divided into three levels. During the first two levels, from six to seven and eight to ten years, education is general and normally given by a single teacher. In the final level, from 11 to 13, the curriculum is divided into different areas of study taught by specialists.

Those who complete the course satisfactorily are awarded the *Título de Graduado Escolar* which is a prerequisite for further education leading to university. Those who do not receive the *Título* are given the *Certificado de Escolaridad*. This can be used for entrance to technical education

Bachillerato Unificado Polivalente

After gaining the *Título de Graduado Escolar*, pupils will normally study from the age of 14 to 16 for the *Bachillerato Unificado Polivalente* (BUP), a three-year academic course designed to lead to higher education or higher level technical studies. The qualification at the end of the period is the *Título de Bachiller* which may be used to enter second level technical studies or attend a one-year pre-university course, the *Curso de Orientación Universitaria* (COU).

Technical education

Alongside the higher education system designed to lead to university or 'higher technical' classes there is a 'technical' education system with a strong practical bent for the less gifted which takes pupils from the age of 14. The first level of technical education is for children who failed to gain the *Título de Graduado Escolar*. The second level is for holders of the BUP or those who have completed the first level of technical education. A third higher level of technical education is planned but not yet implemented.

Spanish universities

The majority of Spanish pupils who complete secondary education go on to university – as many as 75 per cent according to Government figures. There are 29 state universities and four private universities in Spain. Entrance is normally restricted to those who have passed the COU and a university entrance examination. Mature students and those who have followed high level technical courses can also be accommodated, however. The first university level consists of three years and leads to a diploma. A further two years of specialised study is necessary before the awarding of a degree, the *licenciatura*. Students may then continue to work for their doctorate.

Further education

Spain has its own equivalent of Britain's Open University, the *Universidad Nacional de Educación a Distancia*, which has made higher education available to a wide section of the population. In addition, resorts and towns normally have busy evening and afternoon adult education centres offering inexpensive courses in a wide range of fields.

HEALTH AND WELFARE

Health is a subject which is often overlooked by those thinking of moving to Spain. The climate seems so beneficial that medical matters may be overlooked. Do not be deceived. Illness and old age are not dispelled by the sun.

Retirement

Many retired couples are now attracted to permanent homes in Spain. The warm climate leads to lower fuels bills during the winter, and state pensions can, through EEC rules, now be collected at Spanish post offices. You can claim state pension either as a temporary visitor to the country or as a resident. In the latter case, you will be paid the UK pension or the Spanish, whichever is the higher.

Retirement in Spain can be a fulfilling experience for those who approach the subject knowledgeably. But it is no paradise for the elderly. There are the same fears of street crime in the large cities which one will find in almost any Western country. Loneliness is a common problem for retired couples who fail to integrate into one of the social organisations for foreigners in tourist areas. And the one certain event which all will face – the loss of a partner – is rarely considered with any degree of frankness when the initial decision is made. This is a serious mistake, and may lead to the surviving partner spending a miserable life in an idyllic coastal location, lacking close friends and the increasingly essential everyday acts of assistance which are needed by everyone in old age. Some of the saddest foreign residents of Spain are those who abandoned everything in Britain for a new life in the sun, only to discover later that the closeknit family of friends and relationships they had taken for granted at home was impossible to recreate in a new country.

On the other hand, the canny pensioner can probably spend less on day-to-day living than in Britain, through such measures as reduced winter heating bills and eating wisely, avoiding high price items such as steak and shellfish. Those who do integrate into the friendly organisations of the coastal areas are usually adamant that they are happier than they might have been had they stayed in Britain. Turning retirement into a new lease of life rather than a decline into old age is a challenge anywhere. It can be overcome in Spain just as it can in Britain, and there are many happy pensioners to prove it. But you must be realistic about the future. Do not buy a property which may be difficult to live in when mobility becomes less easy. Have a good physical check-up before you leave so that you are aware of any health problems, and make sure that you know how to get continuing treatment for any illnesses which are already apparent.

Finally, plan for an *active* Spanish retirement, not a sedentary one. Nothing is more guaranteed to age the Mediterranean pensioner than a daily round of lazy mornings, afternoon siestas and excessive evening meals... as any Spanish pensioner will quickly tell you.

Alcohol abuse

Alcohol made in Spain is much cheaper than its British equivalent, with domestic spirits being particularly inexpensive. A bottle of Spanish brandy costs as much as a bottle of table wine in Britain. Imported drinks, however, are more expensive. Whether it is the price difference or the readiness of Spanish bars to stay open all hours is irrelevant. The plain fact is that alcohol abuse is a growing problem among the expatriate community, as it is in most Western societies.

Common sense is the best way to tackle alcohol abuse. Avoid drinking spirits at lunchtime – the large gin and tonic followed by a siesta syndrome is familiar to all expatriate communities. If your new friends drink more than you, stick to mineral water, mixed with wine if necessary, and don't feel inhibited to say no. Spanish beer is low strength and so carbonated that you are unlikely to be willing to consume so much that it will affect you.

Alcohol abuse is not confined to the expatriate community. Drinking wine or spirits is part of Spanish life; you will often see workers taking a large glass of brandy with their morning coffee, and seas of wine and sherry are consumed at the fairs and fiestas which are liberally dotted throughout the calendar of every Spanish community. The drinks industry is producing a number of new de-alcoholised products and promoting campaigns for sensible drinking. Self-help groups for expatriate alcoholics exist in all the resort areas and advertise in the columns of the local English language press.

Temporary health care in Spain

All citizens of EEC countries are entitled to free or reduced cost *emergency* health care in member nations. You will not receive free treatment for day-to-day medical requirements under these arrangements which are designed for those taking holidays, or temporary residence, in other countries.

In Britain, to qualify for these arrangements you obtain form E111 which is available from any office of the Department of

Health and Social Security. Make your application at least a month before you go, though it will normally be processed across the counter. Treatment under this scheme varies and may be limited in resort areas. The E111 is used to pay for hospital treatment or exchanged at social services offices in Spain for a set of vouchers which can be set against other state medical treatment. You will still be required to pay for prescribed medicines and dental treatment. Visitors to Gibraltar who are UK citizens receive free treatment at St Bernard's Hospital or Casemates Health Centre without the need for an E111.

If you do not have an E111 you will be expected to pay for medical treatment as required. In any case, you should not regard the E111 system as an alternative to travel insurance. The latter is vital, covering you against costs which may not be regarded as emergencies, and for theft and loss of belongings. You may have to pay the bill first and then reclaim the sum from your insurer on your return.

Spanish state health care and contributions

The state health service in Spain has as many critics as its British counterpart. Queues, waiting lists and bureaucracy are an endemic part of the system. The quality of health care itself is variable, as is that of the private health system. Those with complex or serious health problems should make sure that they have access to an English-speaking doctor in their vicinity.

There are a number of state health care benefits which are available to UK citizens living in Spain under reciprocal arrangements negotiated within the EEC. Whatever your status, pensioner or full-time employee, you should register your entitlement and change of residence with the UK state system before you leave. This is done through the Department of Health and Social Security, Overseas Branch, Newcastle-upon-Tyne NE98 1YX. This branch deals with inquiries about health, pension and social security rights within the EEC. When writing to the branch always include your full name, date of birth and, where possible, your national insurance or pension number.

Any UK citizen receiving a state invalidity or retirement pension or widow's benefit who lives in Spain is eligible to free state health service treatment as if he or she were a citizen. You *must* register your change of residence with the DHSS Overseas Branch listed above. They will send you the relevant form which can be used to obtain a Spanish national health card, a *cartilla*, from the Spanish social services. Apply to the DHSS for the application form as soon as you know that you intend to leave the country permanently. The paperwork may take some time to complete and any medical treatment required in the meantime could come straight out of your pocket.

What happens to your National Insurance contributions paid in UK if you move to Spain to work and live? Since both countries are members of the EEC, you can move from member state to member state without losing your social security rights – provided you comply with all the regulations. In other words, moving from Britain to Spain and shifting from UK National Insurance to Spanish social security payments does not lose you British rights. If you return to work in Britain having worked in Spain for several years you will not be asked for the missing years of NI contributions, and vice versa.

Most people who move to Spain to work will already have jobs or be about to launch new businesses. Employment, existing or new, invariably involves the registration of the post with the Spanish social services authorities and the regular payment of insurance fees.

Your UK NI contributions will normally end when you cease residence, and this should be perfectly acceptable to the authorities. It is a good idea to let the DHSS Overseas Branch know that you have moved abroad, preferably in advance with the normal details plus your proposed date of departure and the name and address of any employer for whom you will be working. The authorities may, quite naturally, be suspicious of someone who simply disappears from the country without warning and then returns several years later and attempts to resume work, or claim benefits, with no documentary proof of payment in the intervening time.

There are several exceptions to these general rules, principally for people whose work takes them from country to country. You will find them outlined in leaflet SA29 from the DHSS.

Private insurance

A growing number of foreign residents in Spain now take out private medical insurance in addition to paying state benefits where required. The trend towards private medicine is not confined to Spain. Private medical insurance schemes, pioneered in the US, are enjoying great popularity in most western countries as pressures on state health services increase. A private health scheme does guarantee that you will not have to worry about sizable private health bills if you choose to circumvent the state system in order to get early treatment.

However, no private health scheme is, in truth, a sure way of receiving *better* treatment than the fellow in the next bed. What you get for your monthly instalments is priority, convenience and, in hospitals with private beds, more comfort than might be expected in state wards. You may well find, as in Britain, that you are treated by precisely the same specialists who would attend to you in the state sector.

Health insurance schemes can offer a great deal of comfort, even for those in the best of health. But the fine print of all such contracts needs to be examined carefully, preferably with the help of a good insurance broker. There are no bargains in medical insurance. Each policy has been carefully formulated to bring a profitable return on the monthly premium by weighing up the age of the applicant against the cost of the medical facilities he or she would prefer.

Obviously, the older pay more, since they are the chief users of medical facilities. But you will often find that cheaper insurance policies have loopholes which make them rather expensive, such as a limit on the level of hospital payments, restrictions on the policy outside Spain, and a bar on the free provision of therapeutic medical equipment. These can be very false economies in a country where private beds for specialist treatment may cost more than £1,000 a day.

For those willing to pay, there is a level of health policy aimed at the rich expatriate. These include such facilities as air transport to private hospitals in the patient's home country and, in the case of one Costa del Sòl company, a helicopter ambulance to the nearest hospital.

The UK offices of British clearing banks and financial consultants controlled by FIMBRA are a good source of impartial advice on health insurance schemes. Brokers in Spain should know the field, but remember that all are paid on commission and may have an interest in selling you the most expensive policy on their books.

Bibliography

Lookout, Lookout Publications, Puebla Lucia, 29460, Fuengirola, Málaga, Spain. Tel:(52) 460950, monthly, annual subscription 3,000 pesetas (Spain), £19 or 4,500 pesetas (elsewhere in Europe), $43 or 5,000 pesetas (rest of world), ISSN 0024-6433

Essential English language guide to living in Spain, principally for those who are already there, but an appetiser for anyone thinking of the move. Articles on property trends, Spanish news of interest to foreign residents, travel, food, wine and David Searl's invaluable column on law.

The Costa del Sol Property Guide, Lookout Publications, 600 pesetas, ISSN 0214-3208

Published annually, the guide includes a review of the state of the building sector and news of new housing developments, trends in property prices, furnishings, and facilities for foreign residents. There is a useful list of all coastal developments along the coast. Invaluable for anyone looking on the Costa del Sol, interesting reading for people looking elsewhere.

You and the Law in Spain, David Searl, Lookout Publications, 900 pesetas, ISBN 84-398-4832-3

David Searl has a well-earned reputation as Spain's leading English language writer on Spanish law. The book reflects some of the topics discussed in his monthly column in *Lookout* magazine, often from readers' inquiries. As the author stresses, the book is not a substitute for professional advice, but it is a worthwhile legal 'bible' for anyone thinking of spending more than the odd holiday in Spain.

Working Abroad, the Daily Telegraph Guide to Working and Living Overseas, Godfrey Golzen, Kogan Page, £7.95, ISBN 1-85091-519-9

A comprehensive guide tailored specifically to the needs of people who are posted abroad by their companies. The section on Spain is short; most of the book concentrates on contractual, financial, social and family advice for people who eventually aim to return to the UK.

Spain's Hidden Country, A Traveller's Guide to Northern Spain, Frank Barrett and Chris Gill, Telegraph Publications, £4.95, ISBN 0-86367-069-5

One of the few modern guides to northern Spain. Excellent advice on where to find the most interesting inland and coastal resorts, with hotel and restaurant recommendations from Galicia to the Picos de Europa.

Most resort areas have some kind of English language weekly newspaper, often given away free in hotels and shops. Such publications contain lists of estate agents and private property advertisements. The best English language newspaper in Spain is Mallorca's *Daily Bulletin*, which is published six times weekly and is a useful guide to local life and property markets.

Sources of Information

These details were supplied by the organisations concerned in mid-1989. Telephone numbers and addresses may have changed during or since publication.

BRITISH GOVERNMENT REPRESENTATION IN SPAIN

Madrid
British Embassy, Calle de Fernando el Santo 16, Madrid 4.
Tel: 419-0200.

Seville
British Consulate, Plaza Nueva 8 (Dpdo). Tel: 228875.

Alicante
British Consultate, Plaza Calvo Sotelo 1/2 – 1 Apartado de Correos 564, Alicante 1. Tel: 216190/216022.

Barcelona
British Consulate-General, Edificio Torre de Barcelona, Avenida Diagonal 477 (13th Floor), 08036 Barcelona. Tel: 322-2151.

Tarragona
British Consulate, Calle Real 33, 1° 1a, 43004 Tarragona.
Tel: 220812.

Bilbao
British Consulate-General, Alameda de Urquijo 2-8, Bilbao 8.
Tel: 4157600.

Santander
British Consulate, Paseo de Pereda 27. Tel: 220000.

Las Palmas, Gran Canaria
British Consulate, Edificio Cataluna, C/Luis Morote 6, Third Floor, 35007 Las Palmas (PO Box 2020). Tel: 262508.

Santa Cruz de Tenerife
British Consulate, Plaza Weyler 8-1°, Santa Cruz de Tenerife 38003. Tel: 286863.

Lanzarote
British Consulate, Calle Rubicon 7, Arrecife. Tel: 815928.

Málaga
British Consulate, Edificio Duquesa, Calle Duquesa de Parcent 4.
Tel: 217517/212325.

Vigo
British Consulate, Plaza de Compostela 23-6° (Aptdo 49).
Tel: 437133.

Palma de Mallorca
British Consulate, Plaza Mayor 3D, Palma de Mallorca 2, Mallorca 07002. Tel: 712445/712085/716048.

Ibiza
British Vice-Consulate, Avda Isidoro Macabich 45-1°, Apartado 307, 07800 Ibiza. Tel: 301818/303816.

Menorca
British Vice-Consulate, Torret 28, San Luis, Menorca. Tel: 366439.

SPANISH GOVERNMENT ORGANISATIONS IN LONDON

Visas should be obtained from the Spanish Consulate. Holders of passports issued by the governments of the EEC, YSA and Japan do not need a visa for visits to Spain up to 90 days in length. The Consulate also deals with inquiries about work permits.

Spanish Consulate, 20 Draycott Place, London SW3.
   Tel: 01-581 5921.
Spanish Embassy, 24 Belgrave Square, London SW1X 8QA.
   Tel: 01-235 5555.
Agricultural Attaché of the Spanish Embassy, 1st-2nd Floor, 54 Upper Montague Street, London W1H 1ST. Tel: 01-723 9967.
Commercial Office of the Spanish Embassy, 22 Manchester Square, London W1. Tel: 01-486 0101.
Labour Attaché of the Spanish Embassy, 20 Peel Street, London W8. Tel: 01-221 0098.
Spanish Chamber of Commerce, 5 Cavendish Square, London W1. Tel: 01-637 9061.
Spanish Institute/Cultural Attaché, 102 Eaton Square, London SW1. Tel: 01-235 1485.
Spanish Promotion Centre (Food and Wine from Spain), 22 Manchester Square, London W1. Tel: 01-935 6140.

SPANISH BANKS IN LONDON

Banco de Bilbao, 100 Cannon Street, London EC4.
 Tel: 01 623-3060.
Banco Central, 82 London Wall, London EC2. Tel: 01-588 0181.
Banco Exterior UK, 60 London Wall, London EC2.
 Tel: 01-628 8714.
Banco de Sabadell, 27 Wood Street, London EC2. 7AL.
 Tel: 01-606 4297.
Banco de Vizcaya, 58-60 Moorgate, London EC2.
 Tel: 01-920 0121.
Banco Pastor, Burne House, High Holborn, London WC1.
 Tel: 01-242 0478.
Banco de Santander, 10 Moorgate, London EC2. Tel: 01-606 7766.
Banco Hispano-Americano, 15 Austin Friars, London EC2N 2DJ.
 Tel: 01-268 4499.
Banco de Galicia, 41 Crutched Friars, London EC3.
 Tel: 01-480 5086.

BRITISH BANKS IN SPAIN

BARCLAYS BANK SA
There are approximately 130 branches of Barclays in Spain (1989), both in tourist resorts and in inland towns serving Spanish customers. Only those in resort areas are listed.

Head Office
Barclays Bank, Plaza de Colón 1, Madrid (postal address:
 Apartado de Correos 1075, 28080 Madrid). Tel: 4102800.

Costa del Sol
Benalmadena-Costa. Edificio Centro Comercial Olé, Ctra Cádiz-Málaga Km229, 29630 Benalmadena.
 Tel: 444846. Manager: M Cañestro.
Estepona. Avenida de España 300, 29680 Estepona. Tel: 803854.
 Manager: P Giranés.
Fuengirola. Avda Suel s/n, Puebla Lucia, Edificio Maria Luisa, 29640 Fuengirola. Tel: 460058. Manager: F Pozo.

Marbella. Avda Ricardo Soriano 68, 29600 Marbella. Tel: 776550.
Manager: CR White.
Mijas (Costa). Edificio Calypso 2, Urbanización Calypso, Ctra
Cádiz-Málaga Km 197.6, 29650 Mijas (Costa).
Tel: 831343/831344.
Mijas (Pueblo). Avda de Méjico 6, Mijas Pueblo 29650.
Tel: 485300. Manager: LF Pozo.
Nueva Andalucia. Ctra Cádiz-Málaga 174, Edificio Iberico,
Nueva Andalucia 29660. Tel: 810053. Manager: Miss AC
Maestre.
San Pedro de Alcántara. Urbanización Guadalmina, Ctra Cádiz-
Málaga Km 170, 29678 San Pedro de Alcántara.
Tel: 786550/786554. Manager: S Bethencourt.
Sotogrande. Centro Comercial, Cortijo Los Canos, Sotogrande,
San Roque 11310 Cádiz. Tel: 792266. Manager: I Delclaux.

Balearic Islands
Palma de Mallorca. Main branch, Avda Alejandro Rosello 15,
07002 Palma de Mallorca. Tel: 727582/727131. Manager: F
Tous.
Portals Nous. Edificio Alkaid, Portals Nous 07015. Tel:
675512/675525. Manager: MJ Herracz.
Menorca. Sant Jordi 31, 07702 Mahon, Menorca. Tel: 368131.
Manager: J Barber.

Canary Islands
Tenerife. Complejo Garden City, Locales 1 y 2, Playa de Las
Américas, 38660 Adeje, Tenerife. Tel: 793062/793207.
Manager: JL Menchero.
Santa Cruz de Tenerife. Plaza de Weyler 8, 38003 Santa Cruz de
Tenerife. Tel: 285266.
Gran Canaria. Presidente Alvear 25, 35007 Las Palmas.
Tel: 263354. Manager: A Caballero de Rodas. Avda de Italia 7,
35290 Playa de Inglés, Las Palmas. Tel: 370022. Manager: M
Santana.

Costa Blanca
Moraira. Ctra de Teulada-Moraira Km 5, 7, 03724 Teulada.
Tel: 745198. Manager: LA Sanz.

Jávea. Ctra Cabo La Nao Km 3.2, 03730 Jávea. Tel: 770112.
   Manager: SH Mackenzie.
Alicante. Alfonso X, El Sabio 43, 03001 Alicante. Tel: 219565.
   Manager: JL Lérida.

NATIONAL WESTMINSTER
National Westminster is represented in Spain by Banco NatWest March which has more than 160 branches in 22 provinces of the mainland. An up-to-date list of branches is available from the Marketing Manager, European Businesses, National Westminster Bank PLC, 10-11 Old Broad Street, London EC2N 1BB. Tel: 01-920 5975.

Madrid (Head Office). Miguel Angel 23, 28010. Tel: 4191112.
Barcelona (Principal Office): Calle Caspe 17, 08010. Tel: 3174658.

Costa del Sol
Málaga. Alameda Principal 51. Tel: 213627.
Benalmadeña. Avda Antonio Machado, Conjunto Alay.
   Tel: 561911.
Estepona. Avda España 174. Tel: 790227.
Fuengirola. Avda Suel 4. Tel: 479200.
Marbella. Avda Ricardo Soriano s/n. Tel: 823737.
Nueva Andalucia. Centro Comercial Plaza. Tel: 817002.
San Pedro de Alcantara. Plaza Vista Alegre s/n. Tel: 783550.
Seville. Madrid 1. Tel: 326563
Jerez de la Frontera. Beato Juan Grande 11. Tel: 326563.

Costa Blanca
Alicante. Calle Angel Lozano 13, 03001. Tel: 141144.
Denia. Calle Patricio Fernandez, Esquina Calle Sagunda.
   Tel: 789712.

Costa Brava
Blanes. Carrer Ample 2. Tel: 336213.
Lloret de Mar. Paseo Agustin Font 16. Tel: 365726.

MIDLAND BANK
Madrid. Calle José Ortega y Gasset 29-1, 28006. Tel: 4310613.
   Contact: F Gonzales-Robatto.

INTERNATIONAL SCHOOLS IN SPAIN

The European Council of International Schools, 21b Lavant Street, Petersfield, Hants GU32 3EL, tel: 0730 68244, maintains a list of international schools in Spain and other countries. The following schools operate UK curricula at the time of writing. Details of schools with other curricula are available from the Council. Fees are stated per term and vary for day pupils and boarders and according to age.

Barcelona
Kensington School, Ctra de Esplugas, 86 bis (Pedralbes), Barcelona 34. Tel: 2035457. Headmaster: EP Giles. Age range 5-18, fees Ptas 405,000-546,000.
Oak House School, San Pedro Claver 12-18, Barcelona 08017. Headmaster: Pelegrin Viader. Age range 3-17. Fees Ptas 287,000-416,000.
St Peter's School, Eduard Toldra 14-18, Pedralbes, Barcelona 08034. Tel: 2043612. Headmistress: Joy Headland. Age range 3-18. Fees Ptas 450,000-630,000.

Bilbao
Izarra International College, Finca Arguitza, 01440 Izarra, Alava. Tel: 45437100. Headmaster: John P Caselaw. Age range 4+-18. Fees Ptas 150,000-420,000.

Cádiz
English Centre, Aptdo Correos 85, Ctra Fuentebrava KM 1.2, El Puerto de Santa María, Cádiz 11500. Tel: 850560. Headmistress: Linda M Randell. Age range 3-14. Fees Ptas 163,250.

Madrid
English Montessori School, Eduardo Vela No 10 Aravaca, Madrid 28023. Tel: 4574222/2070305/2071542. Headmaster: Norman Roddom. Age range 3-14. Fees Ptas 220,000-300,000.
Hastings School, Paseo de la Habana 204, Madrid 28036. Tel: 2590621. Headmistress: Helen Pennefather. Age range 3-14. Fees Ptas 228,000.

International College, Spain, Aptdo 271, 28100 Alcobendas.
Tel: 6502398. Director: DA Kirkwood. Age range 3-18. Fees
Ptas 240,000-855,000.

International Primary School, Rosa Jardón 3, Madrid 28016.
Tel: 2592121/2590722. Principal: Anne Mazón. Age range 3-14.
Fees Ptas 210,000-390,000.

King's College, Paseo de los Andes, Soto de Viñuelas, El Goloso.
Tel: 8034800. Headmaster: Peter Stokes. Age range 3-19. Fees
Ptas 270,000-513,000.

Numont School, Calle Parma 16, Madrid 28043. Tel: 2002431.
Principal: M Ann Swanson. Age range 2-11. Fees Ptas 276,000-308,000.

Runnymede College, Calle del Arga 9, El Viso, Madrid 28002.
Headmaster: Arthur F Powell. Age range 3-18. Fees Ptas
225,000-634,000.

Costa del Sol

Aloha College, El Angel, Nueva Andalucia, Marbella.
Tel: 814133/812729. Director: John F Poppleton. Age range 3-18. Fees Ptas 273,000-465,000.

International School at Sotogrande, Aptdo 15, Sotogrande. Tel:
792902. Principal: Rosemary Ridley de Gomez. Age range 3-16. Fees Ptas 264,000-369,000.

Sunny View School, Aptdo 175, Cerro de Toril, Torremolinos.
Tel: 383164. Principal: Jane Barbadillo. Age range 4-18. Fees
Ptas 205,000-350,000.

Other coastal regions

El Plantio International School of Valencia, Urbanización El
Plantio, Calle 233 s/n, La Cañada, Valencia. Tel: 1321410.
Headmistress: Janet E Juett. Age range 3-9. Fees Ptas 300,000.

Sierra Bernia School, San Rafael s/n, Alfaz del Pi, Alicante 03580.
Tel: 5889449. Headmaster/Director: Duncan M Allan. Age
range 3-18. Fees Ptas 180,000-330,000.

Mallorca

The Academy – English Preparatory School, Aptdo 1300, Palma
de Mallorca. Tel: 600538. Principal: Mrs CA Walker. Age
range 3-13. Fees 180,000-360,000.

Baleares International School, Cami Son Toells y Calle Cabo
  Mateu Coch 17, San Agustin, 07015 Palma de Mallorca.
  Tel: 401812. Director: Barrie Wiggins. Age range 3-19.
  Fees US$1,500-5,000.
Bellver International College, 10 José Costa Ferrer, Palma 07015.
  Tel: 401679. Principal: Jean McShane. Age range 3-18. Fees
  Ptas 199,000-424,000.
Queen's College, the English School, Juan de Saridakis 64, Palma
  de Mallorca. Tel: 401011. Headmaster: F Holmes. Age range 3-
  18. Fees Ptas 165,000-363,000.

Canary Islands
British School of Grand Canary, PO Box 11, Tafira Alta, Las
  Palmas. Tel: 351167. Headmaster: R Kerry Williams. Age
  range 4-16. Fees Ptas 192,000-267,000.
British Yeoward School, Parque Taoro, Puerto de la Cruz,
  Tenerife. Tel: 384685. Headmaster: Martin J Weston. Age
  range 3-16. Fees Ptas 126,000-173,000.

LAWYERS

The UK Law Society can supply a list of members who have experience of Spanish law. However, this is incomplete and some of those mentioned may be experienced in commercial, not residential law. If you already have a solicitor in England, his practice may well know a lawyer with some experience of Spanish property transactions.
The Law Society, 113 Chancery Lane, London WC2A 1PL.
Tel: 01-242 1222.

BRITISH-LINKED ACCOUNTANTS IN SPAIN

The Institute of Chartered Accountants, Gloucester House, 399 Silbury Boulevard, Central Milton Keynes MK9 2HL, tel: 0908 668833, supplies a list of members and associated firms. This costs £17 post free to members or £25 post free to non-members. A topographical breakdown is available for £7.50 post free. Members in tourist areas in Spain include:

Alicante
Grant Thornton International, Pintor Cabrera 22-4b, 03003.
P B James, Casa Tarica, Bujon 372, Calle Santiago de Compostela.

Barcelona
Arthur Andersen & Co, Avinguda, Diagonal 654, 08034.
Arthur Young & Co, Spanish Firm Diagonal 618, 08021.
Coopers & Lybrand, Edificio Heron, Diagonal 601 10a 08028.
Grant Thornton International, Edificio Barcino Tuset 20-24 08006.
KPMG Peat Marwick, Edificio Masters, Pedro I Pons 9-11 08034.
Price Waterhouse, Torre Catalunya, Avda de Roma 2 & 4 08014

Cádiz
M J Humphries, Calle Buenos Aires 2, Sotogrande.
T J Revill, Galerias Paniagua 20, Sotogrande.

Málaga
Arthur Andersen & Co, Hilera 8 29007.
Coopers & Lybrand, Alameda de Cólon 9-6 29001.
B J Northcott, Servi-Center, Terraza 4, 29680 Estepona.

Palma de Mallorca
Camps, Brown & Associates, Calle Honderos 1-3B.
Ernst & Whinney, Edificio Minaco, Avda Alejandro Rosello 15-2.
Mehdizadeh, Pasaje Santa Catalina, Siena 1, Edificio Olivar.

Las Palmas, Gran Canaria
Ernst & Whinney, Triana 120 35002

Santa Cruz de Tenerife
Ernst & Whinney, Edificio Hamilton, Oficina 26, Calle la Marina 7.
Price Waterhouse, Edificio Hamilton, Oficina 81, Calle la Marina 7.

ESTATE AGENTS

There are two professional bodies for estate agents in Great Britain, the Royal Institution of Chartered Surveyors and the

National Association of Estate Agents. Both maintain lists of members who specialise in Spain. Names of members are carried here as information, not as recommendations.

Members of the Royal Institution of Chartered Surveyors, 12 Great George Street, Parliament Square, London SW1. Tel: 01-222 7000.

London
Chesterton Prudential, 116 Kensington High Street, London W8 7RW. Tel: 01-937 7244.
Hampton & Sons, 6 Arlington Street, St James's, London SW1A 1RB. Tel: 01-493 8222.
Russell-Cowan, 38 Albemarle Street, London W1X 3FB. Tel: 01-493 5565.
Sturgis & Son, 140 Park Lane, London W1Y 4DN.
 Tel: 01-493 2732. Also at: Sturgis International, 5 Avenida de Arias, Maldonado, Marbella, Málaga, Spain. Tel: 777090.

Provinces
Bailey-Ambler International, Westgate House, 30 Westgate, Grantham, Lincs NG31 6QQ. Tel: 0476 62525.
Bradley & Vaughan Overseas, 34/36 Broadway, Haywards Heath, Sussex RH16 3AL. Tel: 0444 412551.
Hamptons, 103/105 Promenade, Cheltenham, Glos GL50 1NR. Tel: 0242 514849.
Hispano Wessex Property, The Downes, Exbourne, Okehampton, Devon EX20 3RP. Tel: 0837 85291.
Halifax Property Services, 52 Perrymount Road, Haywards Heath, Sussex RH16 2AL. Tel: 0444 459961.
Shipways, 172 High Street, Harborne, Birmingham B17 9PP. Tel: 021 427 3264.
Kenneth Ward & Co, Exchange House, 77 Laleham Road, Staines, Middx TW18 2EA. Tel: 0784 464151.
Chilcott, White & Co (Overseas), 125 South End, Croydon CR9 1AR. Tel: 01-688 4151. Also at: Oficina Urbanizacíon Las Cuevas, La Orotava, Tenerife, Canary Islands.
SA Draycott, The Old Bank House, 68 High Street, Lymington, Hants SO4 9AL. Tel: 0590 673282. Also at: S A Draycott, José

Feliu Estate Agents, Av. del Mar 12, Edificio Port Royal 6,
Palma de Mallorca, Baleares.
Vernon Smith European 38 Bell Street, Reigate, Surrey RH2 7BA.
Tel: 0737 46868. Also at: Vernon Smith European, Conjunto
Casana, Block B, Via 1, Nueva Andalucia, Marbella, Málaga,
Spain. Tel: 810695. With associated offices in the Costa Blanca,
Mallorca and Ibiza.

Mainland Spain
FR Jacobson, El Mirador, Cortijo La Guapa, La Mamola,
Granada. Tel: 646441.

Gibraltar
Brian Francis & Associates Ltd, Unit S, Don House, 30/38 Main
Street, Gibraltar (for properties in Andalucia). Tel: 79889.

Balearic Islands
Tufnell International, Plaza de Carmen 3, Mahon, Menorca,
Baleares. Tel: 364816.
CG Hunt, Investment Services Consultants, Apartado 51, Soller,
Mallorca, Baleares. Tel: 630006.

Canary Islands
Lanzarote Properties, Apartado 228, Arrecife, Lanzarote, Canary
Islands. Tel: 810224.
Property Manager SA, Plaza San Antonio, Playa de los Pocillos,
Lanzarote, Canary Islands. Tel: 826020.

The following are members of the National Association of Estate
Agents, Arbon House, 21 Jury Street, Warwick CV34 4EH. Tel:
0926 496800. Special areas are given at the end of the entry.

DL Headland, Headland Overseas, 67 Wellingborough Road,
Rushden, Northants NN16 7ES. Tel: 0933 53333. *East coast*
J Caswell, Homes in the Sun Ltd, 37 The Headlands, Kettering,
Northants. Tel: 0536 84343. *Costa Blanca*
J Compass, John Compass Ltd, 142 Rose Street, Edinburgh.
Tel: 031 225 5166. *Costa del Sol* and *Mallorca*
RJ Coope, Coope & Co (Properties), 66/67 High Street,
Lymington, Hants. Tel: 0590 677971. *Costa del Sol* and *Mallorca*

SOURCES OF INFORMATION — PROPERTY

JWP Lambie, Villa Antonita, La Isleta, Campello, Alicante, Spain. Tel: 965 632276. *Costa Blanca*

PB Robinson, Sol Spanish Property, 1 Market Street, Bingley, Yorks. Tel: 0274 551101. *Eastern Costa del Sol, Southern Costa Blanca*, resales and lettings

JA Alexander, Alexanders, 174 Edmund Street, Birmingham B3 2HD. Tel: 021 236 4422. *All areas*

Mrs E Lomas, Holkers Estate Agents, The Avenue, Leigh, Lancs. Tel: 0942 671129. *Costa del Sol and Torre del Mar*

M Watson, Calle Virgen de la Nonanova 28, Genova, Mallorca. Tel: 400566. *Mallorca*

I Edwards, Edwards Estate Agents, 2 High Street, Lanark, Scotland ML11 7EX. Tel: 0555 61430/9. *Costa del Sol commercial and residential*

KA Ferguson, Vernon Smith European, 24 High Street, Reigate, Surrey RH2 9AY. Tel: 0737 246868. *Costa Blanca, Costa del Sol, Ibiza* and *Mallorca, commercial and residential*

NE Bailey, Spanish Property Centre, Compton Avenue, Luton, Beds LU4 9AX. Tel: 0582 491140. *Costa Blanca*

KO Arton, Chalcross Estate Agents, 18 Market Place, Chalfont St Peter, Bucks SL9 9EA. Tel: 0753 886335.

Mr Les Allen, B G Balderson Estates, 15 Figtree Lane, Sheffield S1 2DJ. Tel: 0742 752225. *Costa del Sol, Costa Blanca, Tenerife*

Peter Lee, 1 Silver Street, Wiveliscombe, Somerset TA4 2PA. Tel: 0984 24055. *Costa Blanca* and *Costa del Sol*

RM Wilson, Charles E Spalding (Properties), 11 Whitehall Crescent, Dundee, Tayside DD1 4AY. Tel: 0382 29446. *Costa Brava*

S Emmett, Whiteway Properties, Suite 2, 12 High Street, Knaresborough, N Yorks HG5 0EQ. Tel: 0423 865892. *Costa Blanca* and *Costa del Sol*

Trevor Greenhalf, Windsor Estate Agents, 23 Church Street, Rushden, Northants NN10 9YU. Tel: 0933 55124. *Costa Blanca*

MA Rippin, Rippin Overseas, 252A Lincoln Road, Millfield, Peterborough, Cambs. Tel: 0733 53706. *Costa Blanca* and *Costa Calida*

CF Huskisson-Hughes, 12 Foxley Close, Lymm, Cheshire WA13 0BS. Tel: 092 575 6851. *Costa del Sol* and *Costa Calida*

D Ware, Ware & Co, 53 Bridge Street, Taunton, Somerset TA1 1TP. Tel: 0823 259604. *Cabrera-Almeria*

David Doyle, 167 High Street, Berkhamsted, Herts.
  Tel: 0442 86 5562. *Costa del Sol*
JR Ashbrook, Beresford Adams, The Cross, Chester, Cheshire
  CH1 1 NP. Tel: 0244 42101. *Mallorca, Menorca,* and *Ibiza*
CDJ Turner, Dixons Estate Agents, 10 Church Green East,
  Redditch, Worcs B98 8BP. Tel: 0527 585808. *Mainland Spain,
  Mallorca* and *Tenerife*

There are also several independent agents, of whom the oldest established is:

Tithebarn Babet Ltd, 14 High Street, Godalming, Surrey
  GU7 1DL. Tel: 04868 28523. *Mainland Spain and islands*

TIMESHARE

Timeshare Developers Association
23 Buckingham Gate, London SW1E 6LB. Tel: 01-821 8845.

The trade organisation for the UK-based timeshare industry which is the principal developer of timeshare in Spain. Imposes financial and business conditions on members and runs an independent arbitration service between customers and timeshare development owners.

TDA-REGISTERED SPANISH DEVELOPMENTS

Marbella
Marbesa Village, Club Algaida, Club Oasis Marbesa, Club San
  Antonio: Atlantic Leisure Group, 1 Grosvenor Gardens Mews
  North, Ebury Street, London SW1W 0JT. Tel: 01-823 6723.
Dona Lola Club, Leila Playa Club: Barratt International Resorts,
  Consort House, Consort Way, Horley, Surrey RH6 7AF. Tel:
  0293 785144.
Jardines del Puerto, Puerto Banus: JDP Services UK, Unit 517,
  Butlers Wharf Business Centre, 45 Curlew Street, London SE1
  2ND. Tel: 01-407 5065.
Miraflores Club: Miraflores Holdings, 116 College Road,
  Harrow, Middlesex HA1 1BQ. Tel: 01-863 0811.

SOURCES OF INFORMATION — PROPERTY

Estepona
Villacana Club: Barratt International Resorts, Consort House, Consort Way, Horley, Surrey RH6 7AF. Tel: 0293 785144.
Benavista: Wimpey Leisure, 27 Hammersmith Grove, London W6 7EN. Tel: 01-748 2000.

Málaga
Sunset Beach Club: Sunset Development, 29 Fitzwilliam Place, Dublin 2, Eire. Tel: Dublin 612873.

Gran Canaria, Canary Islands
Club Excelsior II, Playa des Ingles, Avda de Tirajana 8, Gran Canaria. Tel: 762425.

Tenerife, Canary Islands
Sunset Bay, Sunset Harbour: Global Development, 9 Melbourne Street, Royston, Herts SG8 7BP. Tel: 0763 248741.
Las Rosas, Los Claveles, El Marques, Sueno Azul: Wimpey Leisure, 27 Hammersmith Grove, London W6 7EN. Tel: 01-748 2000.

Lanzarote, Canary Islands
Las Casitas, Las Brisas: Wimpey Leisure, 27 Hammersmith Grove, London W6 7EN. Tel: 01-748 2000.

PROPERTY SHARING ORGANISATIONS
RCI Europe Ltd., 19-28 Wilton Road, London SW1V 1LW. Tel: 01-821 6622 (members inquiries), 01-821 5588 (other inquiries).
Interval International, Gilmoora House, 57-61 Mortimer Street, London W1N 7TD. Tel: 01-631 1765.

THE SPANISH NATIONAL TOURIST OFFICE

A wide range of tourist brochures is stocked by the London branch of the national tourist office, and the staff can offer general advice to visitors. A stamped addressed envelope is appreciated with requests for leaflets.

Spanish National Tourist Office, 57/58 St James's Street, London SW1A 1LD. Tel 01 499 1901/6.

SPANISH TOURIST DEPARTMENTS AND OFFICES

Most Spanish regions have two levels of tourist organisations – provincial and municipal offices. Municipal offices offer detailed information about the immediate area; provincial offices can supply a range of brochures and maps and will normally hold lists of local estate agents, lawyers and other professionals useful to the potential property buyer.

Andalucia
Dirección General de Turismo, Avda. República Argentina 31, 41071, Seville.
Information offices
Algeciras: Avda. Marina s/n. Tel: 600911.
Almeria: Hermanos Machado s/n, Edificio Servicios Municipales. Tel: 234705.
Baeza: Plaza del Populo s/n. Tel: 740444.
Benalmadeña Costa: Ctra Cádiz-Málaga, km 229. Tel: 442494.
Cádiz: Calderón de la Barca 1. Tel: 211313.
Córdoba: Torrijos 10. Tel: 471235.
Granada: Casa de los Tiros, Pavaneras 19. Tel: 221022.
Huelva: Vásquez Lópex 5. Tel: 257403.
Jaen: Avda. de Madrid 10. Tel: 222737.
La Linea: Avda. 20 de Abril s/n. Tel: 769950.
Málaga Airport: Tel: 312044/316000.
Málaga: Marqués de Larios 1. Tel: 213445/276849.
Marbella: Avda. Miguel Cano 1. Tel: 771442/774693.
Ronda: Plaza de España 1. Tel: 871272.
Seville: Avda. de la Constitución 21. Tel: 221404.

Torremolinos: Bajos de la Nogalera, local 517. Tel: 381578.
Ubeda: Plaza de los Caidos s/n. Tel: 750897.

Aragon
Dirección General de Turismo, Plaza de los Sitios, 7 Zaragoza.
Information offices
Huesca: Coso Alto 35. Tel: 225778.
Teruel: Tomás Nogues 1. Tel: 602279.
Zaragoza: Torreón de la Zuda, Glorieta de Pio X11 s/n.
  Tel: 230027

Asturias
Dirección General de Turismo, Plaza de España 2, 33007 Oviedo.
Information offices
Arenas de Cabrales: Ctre General. Tel: 845284.
Aviles: Ruiz Goméz 21. Tel: 544325.
Cudillero: El Pitu. Tel: 590118.
Gijon: Marqués de San Esteban 1, bajo. Tel: 846046.
Llanes: Nemesio Sobrino. Tel: 400164.
Oviedo: Plaza de Alfonso II el Casto 5. Tel: 213385.

Balearic Islands
Information offices
Ibiza: Paseo Vara del Rey 13, Ibiza. Tel: 301900.
Mallorca: Jaime III, 1, Palma de Mallorca. Tel: 712216.
Menorca: Plaza de la Constitución 13, Mahon. Tel: 363790.

Canary Islands
Dirección General de Turismo, Edificio Usos Multiples,
  c/Arrieta s/n, 35003 Las Palmas de Gran Canaria.
Information offices
Las Palmas, Gran Canaria: Parque de Sta. Catalina. Tel: 264623.
Santa Cruz de Tenerife: La Marina 37. Tel: 287254.
Puerto de la Cruz, Tenerife: Plaza de la Iglesia. Tel: 386000.
Lanzarote: Parque Municipal, Arrecife. Tel: 811860.
Fuerteventura: General Franco 33, Puerto Rosario. Tel: 851024.

Cantabria
Dirección General de Turismo, Plaza Porticada, 19001 Santander.

152 SETTING UP IN SPAIN

Information offices
Laredo: Lopez Seña s/n. Tel: 605492.
Santander: Plaza Porticada 2/n. Tel: 310708.
Santillana: Plaza Mayor s/n. Tel: 818251.

Castilla-La Mancha
Dirección General de Turismo, Cuesta de Carlos V, 10-2, 45071 Toledo.
Information offices
Ciudad Real: Alarcos 31. Tel: 212925.
Cuenca: Dalmacio Garcia Izcara 8. Tel: 222231.
Toledo: Puerta de Bisagra s/n. Tel: 220843.

Castilla-Leon
Dirección General de Turismo, Ctra de Ruieda, Km-3.500, Valladolid 47008.
Information offices
Avila: Plaza de la Catedral 4. Tel: 211387.
Burgos: Plaza de Alonson Martinez 7. Tel: 203125.
Ciudad Rodrigo: Arco de las Amayelas 6. Tel: 460561.
Leon: Plaza de Regla 3. Tel: 237082.
Palencia: Mayor 105. Tel: 740068.
Salamanca: Gran Vía 41. Tel: 243730.
Segovia: Plaza Mayor 10. Tel: 430328.
Soria: Plaza Ramón y Cajal s/n. Tel: 212052.
Valladolid: Plaza de Zorrilla 3. Tel: 351801.
Zamora: Santa Clara 20. Tel: 511845.

Catalonia
Dirección General de Turismo, Paseo de Gracia 105, 08008 Barcelona.
Information offices
Barcelona airport: Tel: 3255829.
Barcelona: Gran Vía de les Corts Catalanes 658. Tel: 3017443.
Gerona: Ciutadans 12. Tel: 201694.
La Junquera: Autopista 17, Zona 14. Tel: 540642.
Lerida: Arc de Pont s/n. Tel: 248120.
Tarragona: Fortuny 4. Tel: 233415.

Valencia
Dirección General de Turismo, Isabel la Católica 8, Valencia 46004.
Information offices – Alicante
Alicante airport: Tel: 285011 ext. 100.
Alicante: Explanada de España 2. Tel: 212285. C/Portugal, 17 Estación Central de Autobuses. Tel: 223802/220700.
Altea: Compte de Altea, Apto 128. Tel: 847434.
Benidorm: Martínez Alejos 16. Tel: 851311/853224. Avda. Panamá s/n. Tel: 856986.
Calpe: Avda. Ejercitos Españoles 66. Tel: 831250.
Cullera: Carrer del Riu 56. Tel: 520974
Denia: Patricio Ferrandiz s/n. Tel: 780957.
Elche: Paseo de la Estacíon, Parque Municipal. Tel: 452747.
Gandia: San José de Calasanz 7. Tel: 873536.
Javea: Plaza Almirante Bastarreche 24. Tel: 790736
Valencia Manises Airport: Tel: 530325.
Valencia: Paz 46. Tel: 524000.

Information offices – Castellon
Benicarlo: Ayuntamiento Municipal, Plaza San Andrés s/n. Tel: 473180.
Benicasim: Paseo Marítimo las Corte. Tel: 300244.
Castellon de la Plana: María Agustina 5, bajo. Tel: 227703.

Extremadura
Dirección General de Turismo, Cárdenas 11, Mérida, Badajoz.
Information offices
Badajoz: Pasaje de Sant Juan 1. Tel: 222763.
Caceres: Plaza General Mola s/n. Tel: 246347.
Caya: Menacho 12. Tel: 222793.
Merida: Puente 9. Tel: 315353.

Galicia
Dirección General de Turismo, Edificio San Caetano, Bloque 5, 28071 Santiago de Compostela.
Information offices
La Coruña: Dársena de la Marina s/n. Tel: 221822.
Lugo: Plaza de España 27-29. Tel: 231361.
Orense: Curros Enriquez 1. Tel: 234717.

Pontevedra: General Mola 1. Tel: 850814.
Santiago de Compostela: Rue del Villar 43. Tel: 584081.
Tuy: Puente Tripes. Tel: 601785.
Vigo: Las Avenidas s/n. Tel: 430577.
Villagarcia de Arosa: Plaza de la Revella 1. Tel: 501008.

La Rioja
Dirección General de Turismo, Gran Vía 41, 26002 Logroño.
Information offices
Logroño: Miguel Villanueva 11, bajo. Tel: 255497.

Madrid
Dirección General de Turismo, Duque de Medinacelli 2, 28014 Madrid.
Information offices
Madrid airport: Tel: 2058656.
Madrid: Princesa, 1 Torre de Madrid. Tel: 2412325.
Aranjuez: Plaza de Santiago Rusinol. Tel: 8910427.
San Lorenzo del Escorial: Floridablanca 10. Tel: 8901554.

Murcia
Dirección General de Turismo, Isidoro de la Cierva, 10-2, 30001 Murcia.
Information offices
Cartagena: Ayuntamiento. Tel: 506483.
Murcia: Alejandro Seiquer 4. Tel: 213716.

Navarra
Dirección General de Turismo, Avenida del Ejercito 2. 31002 Pamplona.
Information offices
Pamplona: Duque de Aliumada 3. Tel: 220748.
Tudela: Plaza de los Fueros s/n. Tel: 821530.

Basque Country
Dirección General de Turismo, Duque de Wellington s/n, 01011 Vitoria.
Information offices
Bilbao: Alameda Mazarredo s/n. Tel: 4326430.
Irun: Puente de Santiago: Tel: 6222239.

Glossary of Useful Terms

Abogado — lawyer
Alquiler — to rent
Aparcamiento — car parking facilities
Apartamento — apartment, flat
Arrendador — landlord
Asesor fiscal — accountant, tax adviser
Autorizacíon de residencia — residency permit
Ayuntamiento — local council, town hall
Billete — banknote
Caja de Ahorros — savings bank
Cocina — kitchen
Comedor — dining room
Comisaría — police station
Comunidad de propietarios — owners' liaison organisation in an *urbanización* or apartment block
Contrato privado — private property contract
Cosas comunes — joint property in a development
Cosas privativas — private property in a development
Cuarto de baño — bathroom
Cuotas de comunidad — contributions to community expenses
Declaracíon de impuesto — tax return
Declaracíon de renta — income tax return
Dirección General de Transaciones Exteriores — regulatory body for foreign exchange transactions
Domiciliación de pagos — bank standing order
Dormitorio — bedroom
Escritura pública — property deed
Finca — country house or mansion

Gestor — clerk who will handle bureaucratic tasks from applying for work permits to registering a change in car ownership
Hacienda — central taxation authority
Hipoteca — mortgage
Honorarios — professional fees
Impuesto de Transmisiones Patrimoniales — property transfer tax payable on private transactions
Impuesto sobre Actos Jurídicos Documentados — stamp duty payable at half a percent if transfer tax is not paid on signature of the *escritura*
Inversion — investment
IVA — Value Added Tax (VAT) payable on property transactions from companies
Letras — instalments plan for paying for purchase
Ley de Costas — the 'law of the coasts' which controls building within the Spanish coastline
Notario — public notary
Parcela — building plot
Patrimonio — inheritance
Permanencia — an extension of 90 days to the original 90-day permit to stay in Spain
Permiso de trabajo — work permit
Plus valía — capital gains tax on rise in value of property, legally the responsibility of the seller, usually paid by the buyer
Propietario — owner
Propina — tip, bonus, gratuity
Registro de la Propiedad — property register
Sala — living room
Saldo — balance of bank account
Seguro — insurance
Seguro de Enfermedad — state health insurance
Seguro obligatorio — compulsory third party car insurance
Seguro voluntario — option car insurance offering better cover up to comprehensive insurance
Talón — bank cheque
Terreno — land
Urbanización — housing development
Vivienda — general term for housing facilities

Index

accountants 52, 104, 108, 118
airlines 6
alcohol abuse 128
Alcudia, Bay of 30
Algeciras 23, 44
Alhaurin El Grande 24
Alicante 39, 41, 42
Almeria 15, 41, 42, 46
Almuñécar 23, 28-9
Alpujarra 15, 24
America, north 76, 82
apartments 13, 67, 105
Arrecife 36
asset tax 117
Andalucia 1, 21, 44
autorizacion de residencia 93

Bachillerato Unificado Polivalente 125
Balearic Islands 1, 30-2
Banco Hipotecario 59-60
Banco Natwest March 57
banks 57, 58, 119, 138-40
Barcelona 32, 38, 42, 43
Barlow Clowes 112, 113
bars 105, 106, 107
Basque country 45
basura 121
Benalmadena 8, 13, 24, 25
Benidorm 39
boats 17
building controls 23
buildings, illegal 61, 63
building societies 57
Bulbion 24
business agencies 102-5
businesses 6, 98, 99, 100:
    starting 101-5, 130
    types of 105-9

Cádiz 44, 45
Cala Blanca 59
Calpe 39
Canary Islands 1, 15, 33-8, 73
Capiléira 24
Carihuela, La 8, 24, 25
Carretera del Muerte 32
Castellon de la Plana 42
cars 12, 14, 15, 23, 96, 97
Cartagena 42
cartilla 130
Casemates Health Centre 129
Castillian 18
Catalan language 18
Catalonia 43
catering 105
Certificado de Escolaridad 125
certificado penal 94
César Manrique 37
Channel Tunnel 6
church schools 124
Coín 15, 24
community fees 67
Conil de la Frontera 43
contribucion urbana 118
copia simple 65
Córdoba 45
Costa Azahar 41-2
Costa Blanca 39-40, 69
Costa Brava 12, 38-9
Costa Calida 42
Costa de la Luz 43-5
Costa del Sol 1, 15, 16, 21-30, 38, 73, 77
Costa Dorada 42-3
Costains 85
cost of living 102
criminal convictions 100

currency exchange 4
Curso de Orientación Universitaria 125, 126

Daily Bulletin 31
debts 59, 60
Defensor del Pueblo 2
Denia 39
DHSS 129, 130
Dirección General de Transacciones Exteriores 100
double taxation 117
drainage 121
driving licences 95-6, 97

E111 form 128, 129
Educación General Básica 125
education 120, 122-6
EEC 96, 100, 121, 126, 128, 129: 1992 4, 55, 91, 98, 109, 119
El Capistrano 13, 29, 51
electricity 122
El Hierro 37
El Puerto de Santa Maria 43
Els Pins Park 59
employing people 100-1
Es Calo 32
escritura de compravento 64, 65, 66, 67
Escuela de Párvulos 124
Es Pujols 32
estate agents 23, 31, 48-9, 50-1, 67, 72, 103, 144-8
estates 13-14, 62, 67
Estepona 23, 27
European Council of International Schools 124
exchange control 55, 56
expatriates, numbers of 1

FIMBRA 113-14, 115, 132
finances 112-19
foreign exchange 65, 94
Foreign Property Owners Institute 53, 67-9
Formentera 32
Frigiliana 29
Fuengirola 23, 25-6

Fuerteventura 15, 34, 37
further education 126

gas 122
Gaudí 13
Gerona 38
gestor 93-4, 96, 97, 99, 100, 118
Gibraltar 15, 23, 28, 44, 116, 129
golf courses 16, 34, 41
Gomera 37
Gran Canaria 33, 34, 35-6

Hacienda 116, 117, 118
health services 94, 126-32
heat pump systems 122
holiday companies 72
holiday homes 9, 10
Horizon 41
Huelva province 44

Ibiza 32
Ilustre Colegio de Abogados 60
Impuesto de Transmisiones Patrimoniales 66
impuesto extraordinario sobre el patrimonio 117
income taxes 116-17
inspección técnica de vehiculos 97
Instituto de Proprietarios Extranjeros 67
Insurance:
    driving 97
    employment 130
    medical 131
interest rates 58
international schools 123-4, 141-2
Interval International 80, 82
investment 10-11, 15, 100, 114
IVA 66, 96, 104

Jardin de Infancia 124
Jávea 39

La Duquesa 23, 28
landlords 71-2
Lanjarón 24
Lanzarote 15, 34, 36-7, 46

La Palma 37
La Sabina 32
Las Palmas 35
Law Society 53
lawyers 49, 50, 52, 58, 60, 68, 99:
    fees 54
    finding 53-4, 143-4
    need for 3, 104
leases 70, 104, 105
ley de costas 63-4
licencia fiscal 100
London Interbank 57
Lookout 5, 68, 69
Lorca 42
Los Boliches 25
Los Cristianos 35

McMillan-Scott, Edward 2, 60, 61, 67, 103
Málaga 21, 25, 28, 30, 41, 44, 45,
Mallorca 14, 15, 18, 31
Marbella 8, 15, 23, 25, 26-7
Marina del Este 29
Mar Menor 42
medicine, private 120, 129
Mediterranean Sea 121
Menorca 32
Mijas 26
Mojácar 41
Montemar 25
MOT 97
motives 6-8
motoring 95-7
Motril 29
moving house 95
municipal taxes 118
Murcia 42

N340 44
National Association of Estate Agents 50
national health card 130
National Insurance 130
Nerja 13, 23, 28-9
Nueva Andalucia 27

offshore funds 115-16
Orgiva 24

Palma 31-2
Peñíscola 42
pensions 126, 127
permanencia 93
pets 95
planning 64
Playa de las Americas 35
Playa de Mitjorn 32
plus valía 66
pollution 121
professions 108-9
property:
    buying 2, 49-50, 52-69
    finding 48-51
    fraud and 2
    investment in 10-11, 15
    laws governing 3, 52-69
    paying for 55-8
    renting 69, 70-2
public services 121-2
Puerto Banus 16, 27
Puerto de la Cruz 35
Puerto del Carmen 36
Puerto del Rosario 37
Puerto de Pollensa 30
Puerto Sherry 43, 44, 62
Punte de la Mona 29

rates 118
RCI 80, 81, 82
registro de la propiedad 65
Reina Sofia airport 35
removal companies 95
rental 6, 69-71
residency, rules 91, 92-4
resorts 8, 12-13, 81
restaurants 105, 106, 107
retirement 9, 10, 126-8
Reus 43
road tax 97
Roquetas de Mar 41
Royal Institute of Chartered Surveyors 50
rubbish collection 121

St Bernard's Hospital 129
sales contract 64-5
Salobreña 23, 29

San Antonia Abad 32
San Fernando 32
San Francisco Javier 32
San Pedro de Alcántara 27-8
Santa Eulalia 32
Searl, David 99
self employment 6, 99, 100
service companies 108
Seville 44
sewage disposal 121
Sitges 43
social security 100
Sociedad Anónima 100
solar heating 122
Sotogrande 14, 23, 28, 51
Spain Today 68, 69
Spanish language 7, 15, 17-18
sports facilities 16-17
stamp duty 65
Svensson, Per 68
swimming pools 16, 120
Switzerland 82

tarjeta communitaria 100
Tarragona 42, 43
taxes 55, 56, 66, 71, 93, 97, 112, 116-18
technical education 125
television 122
temperatures 47
tenants 70-1
Tenerife 33, 34-5
tennis courts 16
Thomson 110, 111
timeshare 6, 34, 38, 39, 41
    advantages 76
    arbitration 87, 89
    club membership 83
    consultation 86
    cooling-off period 85-6
    developer/owner, stature of 84
    disadvantages 75-6
    exchanging 80-3, 87
    finding property 89-90
    freehold 83
    leasehold 83-4
    maintenance charges 75, 79, 86
    marketing 88
    problems 73
    renting and 70, 76-7, 79, 87
    salesmen 74, 75, 109
    selling 78
    service charges 75
    tenure, length of 85
    types of 83-4
    working of 75-6
Timeshare Developers Association 74, 78-9, 85, 87-9
title deeds 65
Título de Bachiller 125
Título de Graduado Escolar 125
Toledo 45
Torremolinos 8, 23, 24-5
Torrevieja 39
tour companies 110
Tourism Department 73-4
tourist development 8
tourist plates 96
tourist retailing 107-8
tourists 92-3
transfer tax 66
traspaso 104
tutoring, private 123

unemployment 100, 109
Universidad Nacional de Educación a Distancia 126
universities 126
urbanizaciónes 58, 61, 62, 72, 121

Valencia 41, 42, 46
VAT *see* IVA
visado de residencia 92, 93, 94, 95, 98, 99, 100
visas 92, 93

water 121
Wimpey 85
work 97-101, 109-11:
    regulations 91, 98-101, 130
    temporary 99, 100
    see also following entry
work permits 4, 94, 98, 99-100, 109, 110

Your Home in Spain 68

Zahara de los Atunes 43, 44

Thinking of Buying in Spain?
£30,000 – £160,000*

*Subject to exchange rate variations

Wimpey have a reputation already recognised for quality and reliability here in the U.K. A reputation that hundreds of people have already relied upon when buying abroad.

We now offer 'Balcon de Bena Vista' and 'Las Palmeras de Bena Vista', midway between Puerto Banus and Estepona, shining examples of luxury homes and pools in the finest location. Adjacent is a superb Gary Player designed championship golf course and nearby are 12 bowling rinks and a tennis club with 13 courts, all managed by Wimpey.

If you would like to know more about Wimpey's developments phone 01 846 2255 (24 hours) or phone Bena Vista, Spain 010 34 52 785799.

WIMPEY LEISURE
Our Reputation is your Guarantee.

Wimpey Leisure, 27 Hammersmith Grove, London W6 7EN
Wimpey Leisure, Centro Commercial KM167, Cadiz-Malaga, Estepona, Malaga, Spain

A puzzle solved...

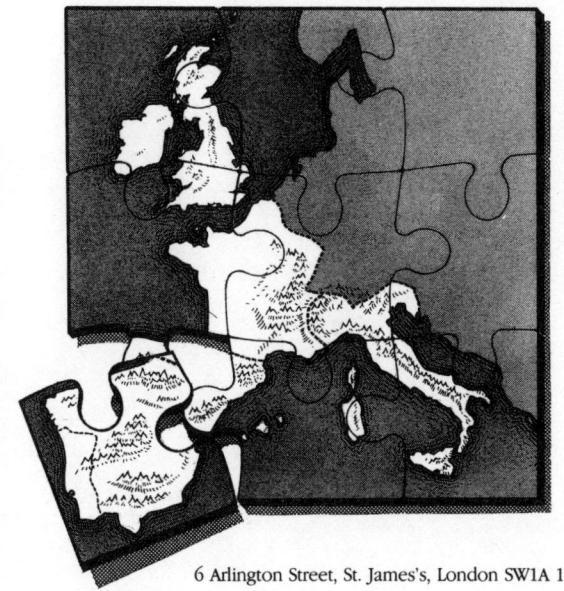

Whether you are a sports enthusiast in search of the sun, or simply in pursuit of an idyllic retreat, we will guide you to the right solution.
Offices throughout mainland Spain and the Balearic Islands.

The European property experts

HAMPTONS INTERNATIONAL
PRIME FORCE IN EUROPEAN PROPERTY

6 Arlington Street, St. James's, London SW1A 1RB. Tel: 01-493 8222. Fax: 01-493 4921

CHARTER PROPERTIES

If you are really serious about
MALLORCA
we offer a superb residential portfolio supervised by our own locally based PR director.

Studios from £8,000, to luxury villas and country mansions.

Huge commercial listings, bars from £20,000, to four star hotels.

We arrange all legal paperwork. Our spanish representative visits the UK every month to answer clients queries re. health, schooling etc.

Charter Properties Warwickshire
We offer the complete service for those who are serious about
MALLORCA

Contact:
**Charter House,
45 High Street, Alcester,
Nr. Stratford on Avon,
Warwickshire B49 5AQ.
Telefax: 0789 764178
Spain: 010-3471-402407. Phone or Fax.**

MAINLAND SPAIN

COSTA BLANCA – Full selection of villas, apartments and plots at Denia, Javea, Moraira, Calpe, Benidorm, *Separate list* south of Alicante incl. Santa Pola and Torrevieja.

COSTA DEL SOL – 3 Separate lists

| Full selection of villas, apartments etc. Malaga–Calahonda incl. Fueneirola. | Puerto Banus, San Pedro de Alcantara, Marbella, Estepona, Sotogrande. | Inland at Alhaurin el Grande and Coin, old and new in quiet fertile valley. |

MOJACAR – New and resale villas, apartments and businesses in this quiet area of south east Spain just 1½ hours drive north of Almeria.

COMPETA/TORROX – 1 hours drive east from Malaga. Choice of new villas or old village houses & fincas for renovation in the hill villages and valleys. All set well back from the coastal strip. Local renovation service.

NERJA – New and resale, on or near the coast, 1 hours drive east of Malaga.

SPANISH ISLANDS

TENERIFE – Choice of new and resale in North & South.
LANZAROTE – Wide choice throughout the island.
MALLORCA – Full range of properties incl. Santa Ponsa, Alcudia, Pollensa.

PORTUGAL

THE ALGARVE – resale or custom built villas, apartments, plots & old farmhouses to renovate coast or inland. *CASCAIS, ESTORIL, SESIMBRA, SINTRA AREAS* – New and resale apartments and villas.
FOZ DO ARELHO – 100kms north of Lisbon around the lagoon and inland. Choice of new and older style properties in quiet locations. *COLMBRA, OPORTO, COSTA VERDE TO SPANISH BORDER* – New and old, coast or inland.

MADEIRA

INCL. PORTO SANTO – Villas/Apartments/Plots.

ITALY

TUSCANY – Wide choice of rural and town properties.
SEPARATE LIST – North of Florence.
UMBRIA – Choice of old to renovate or new.

CYPRUS

Interesting selection. New and old property.

FRANCE

10 sep. lists. – Brittany – stone built properties Dordogne/Lot/Garonne – Perpignan to Pyrenees inland and coast – Charentes inland Angouleme or coast at Royan – Languedoc around Montpelier – Les Trois Vallées ideal for skiing or summer use – Aude/Ariege – app Font Romeu for skiing in Pyrenees – Tarn Valley near Albi.

FLORIDA

THE GULF COAST AND ORLANDO – A wide selection of residential and business properties Visa advice available. *Separate list.* FOR ATLANTIC COAST AND BAHAMAS.

TURKEY

Choice of new and resale in the Bodrum Peninsula.

PLEASE STATE WHICH AREA REQUIRED WITHIN EACH COUNTRY *FOR ENQUIRIES AND FURTHER INFORMATION CONTACT DIRECT:*

BABET

TITHEBARN BABET LTD

14 HIGH STREET, GODALMING, SURREY, GU7 1DL.
TEL (04868) 285253   FAX (04868) 20166

26 YEARS EXPERIENCE IN PROPERTY ABROAD SEARCH, INDEPENDENT ADVICE